ASTOUNDING KNITS!

101
Spectacular
KNITTED CREATIONS
AND Daring
Feats

ASTOUNDING KNITS!

101 Spectacular KNITTED CREATIONS AND Daring Feats

Lela Nargi

Voyageur Press

First published in 2011 by Voyageur Press, an imprint of
MBI Publishing Company, 400 First Avenue North, Suite 300,
Minneapolis, MN 55401 USA

Voyageur Press titles are also available at discounts in bulk quantity for industrial or
sales-promotional use. For details write to Special Sales Manager at MBI Publishing
Company, 400 First Avenue North, Suite 300, Minneapolis, MN 55401 USA.

To find out more about our books, visit us online at
www.voyageurpress.com.

ISBN-13: 978-0-7603-3845-2

Library of Congress Cataloging-in-Publication Data

Nargi, Lela.
  Astounding knits! : 101 spectacular knitted creations and daring feats / Lela Nargi.
     p. cm.
  ISBN 978-0-7603-3845-2 (sb)
  1. Knitting. 2. Knitting--Anecdotes. 3. Knitting--Miscellanea. 4. Curiosities
and wonders. I. Title.
  TT820.N367 2011
  746.43'2--dc22

                             2010026207

Editor: Kari Cornell
Design Manager: Katie Sonmor
Designed by: Mighty Media, Inc.

On the front cover: Photo © NCJ Media
On the title page: Photo © Max Alexander, maxsworld.co.uk
On the back cover:
Untitled (heart lungs, detail), 2007. Courtesy private collection, Sydney, and Dominik Mersch Gallery,
Sydney, photograph by Danny Kildare
A few of York's prickly specimens. Photos by Irene York
Dunbar's happy organic chemistry family. Photos by Anne-Marie Dunbar
A biology experiment gone terribly wooly—Emily Stoneking's Frog.

Printed in China

Contents

Introduction

In the centuries since man (or woman) first thought to
loop together a piece of fabric from two sticks and a piece
of string, all sorts of knitted marvels have appeared on this
planet, from intricate lace and giant carpets to teensy-stitch
socks and patterned counterpanes that could take years to
complete. Thanks to the last decade's renewed enthusiasm
for all things yarny, these marvels are no longer relegated to
annals of history. They're happening right now, all around
us. It's a fabulous time to love knitting!

What qualifies knitting as "astounding"? It could be
something *big*, like Andy Holden's monolithic *Pyramid Piece*.
It could be small, like Annelies de
Kort's micro dog sweaters. It could
be unprecedented, like Dave Cole's
American flag, knit with utility
poles and an excavator. It could be
kooky, like Lauren Porter's life-
size Ferrari. In some instances, it's
extra-smart—see Woolly Thoughts'
mathematical afghans. In others,
it's all about the *idea* behind the
knitting, as in Reknit's recycled
sweater campaign. And in a few
cases, it's actually about *crochet*—invoking the meaning of the
Japanese word *amimono*, which encompasses all crafts fashioned
with string—so we can bring you such boggling innovations as
Daina Taimina's hyperbolic coral. There's even a little history
tucked in among the pages, lest we forget that every innovation
has its roots tucked in to something old.

You'll find artists and crafters and inventors in the pages
of this book, along with a healthy dollop of record-breakers.
Most of all, and all in the name of great fun, you'll find great
knitting!

> It could be
> something *big* …
> small … unprecedented …
> kooky … extra-smart …
> it could be about
> the *idea* behind
> the knitting …

Knitting Small

People have been knitting small for centuries. The folks in this chapter are absolutely in earnest when they refer to their knitting needles as "pins."

1
BUGKNITS

World's Smallest Knitwear!

Smaller than an American dime! Able to fit six miniscule sweaters in a row on one nimble finger! It's a speck! It's a bug! No, it's Bugknits! And it's the smallest knitwear you may ever see (although you'll probably need a magnifying glass in order to truly peruse it in all its detail).

Knitted by Althea Crome, these teensy sweaters are knitted in 1:144 scale. That's a scale that Crome calls "dollhouse for a dollhouse" size. Or, stated more technically and incredibly, eighty stitches per inch. Crome, who designed and knit the somewhat-less-tiny striped gloves and star sweater for the main character in the movie *Coraline*, claims that curiosity is what drove her to find out whether she could create these sweaters—a black and white striped cardigan, a butterfly-sleeved jacket with a luxuriant gold collar, a sweater festooned with a peace symbol—using 100-weight YLI Silk and 200/2 fine Egyptian cotton threads. And, well ... she could. The first experiment was a magenta and yellow jacket, which Crome knit with 50-weight thread.

> "I came across a miniature scarf, and I thought, 'I could try that.'"

continued on page 12

Crome's teensy-weensy sweaters, all in a row. *Photo by Althea Crome, 2004*

Profile
ALTHEA CROME
IN HER OWN WORDS

My miniature knitting evolved from knitting for my children. I had triplets, and I did lots of knitting because I did lots of sitting. Before that, I was knitting for adults. But to make a sweater was so expensive, and so time-consuming, then I'd finish it and the sleeves would be too long. I liked a challenge and wanted to try more complicated things.

Then, when my kids were a few years old, I started building them a dollhouse. It was not interesting, but then I had to furnish it, and I loved the idea of suspended disbelief, not knowing when you looked if the rooms were full-scale. I was reverting to a childhood fascination, a sense of magic and fantasy. I started looking on eBay for furniture and stuff for the dollhouse. I didn't know at the time that there was this whole subset of adults that was obsessed with miniatures. Eventually I came across a miniature scarf, and I thought, 'I could try that.' I started that night. I used baling-weight yarn and size 0 (2mm) needles. The scarf was 2 inches long, but the scale was off—ten or eleven stitches per inch.

Now I work at the proper scale, which is sixty stitches to an inch (except for the nano-knits, which are eighty stitches to an inch). I loved it. It was a total thrill to create an entire garment in one sitting, and designing was the most thrilling part. Eventually, I began to see my knitting as not for dollhouses anymore, or for vignettes. It changed from clothing a doll into a conceptual idea.

My *Scuba Sweater* I knit in order to get out of a funk after my husband and I separated. I had lost my creative juices, and the only thing keeping me afloat, so to speak, was scuba diving. It was a meditative experience. To get my knitting mojo back, I wanted to make a piece of art that reflected what I was experiencing. One day I went scuba diving, and I saw sharks and dolphins. I lost my weight packet and was searching for it in the coral with my diving buddy.

I saw a waterspout, and that's on the back of the sweater in a cabled twist. As you turn the sweater 360 degrees, you see the story. I made a twisted, wavy cast-on so the bottom looks like waves; the collar reflects sea anemones, with bobbles; the buttons were meant to be jewel-like coral. That started me on the pathway to being more conceptual.

All my knitting is done like full-scale knitting—there are no tricks, it's just smaller. People are always shocked and amused because I have big hands, and they sometimes shake, especially when I've had too much coffee. I use surgical stainless steel of varying diameter, cut to the length I want—4, 5, or 6 inches long—then I grind and polish the ends so they are not so pointy that they stab you. I use different silks and wool and cotton. Luckily, I can have a lot of thread in my house and it doesn't take up very much room. I use Biederman silk thread that's 50 weight and YLI silk thread from Japan, which is 100 weight and very fine. I like silk because at this scale, things are very stiff—I like things to be loose and have drape. I've done trades with a Yahoo miniature knitting group—they were a wonderful source of inspiration and camaraderie when I was starting.

I use magnifiers that flip down over my glasses and magnify three and a half times. I'm nearsighted and I can knit without them, but it gives me headaches, and these help the eyestrain and I can knit longer. I knit a lot of Fair Isle and intarsia—I have to take my time and do the stitch, and it takes a little longer. I do drop stitches, but it's okay, I don't panic; I just use a tiny crochet hook to pick it up.

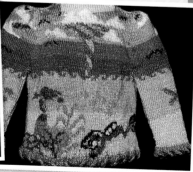

Crome holds her incredible *Scuba Sweater*, seen here from the front …

… and the back. *Photos by Althea Crome, 2008*

continued from page 9

"It was extremely difficult to accomplish," recalls Crome. "The thread kept slipping off the needles, and I nearly gave up the whole enterprise. I designed it as I knit, and it took about a week" to finish. There's only one thing smaller than the astonishingly small creations she makes: the .009 wire Crome uses to stitch them up.

The amazing detail on Crome's *Grecian Urn* sweater. *Photo by Althea Crome, 2007*

MICROKNITS

ANNELIES DE KORT

Unless ...

... you're talking about the even more improbably microscopic knits fashioned by Dutch crafter Annelies de Kort. Fair to say: She's taken nano-knitting one step beyond—to bug on a bug size. She started out as small as Crome, though, with a project in which she created a 1:144 needlework shop diorama that contained a 0.3-inch knitted dress and a 0.2-inch knitted dress, in addition to a bunch of handmade bobbin laces that were smaller than 0.1 inch. After that, she wanted to see if she could knit smaller. Using the hand-dyed #80 to #170 Egyptian cotton that she favors for her nano-lacemaking, de Kort succeeded after "a lot of practice" in creating a 0.2-inch dress and a 0.1-inch sweater. "To make these, I put on my

> Fair to say: She's taken nano-knitting one step beyond—to bug on a bug size.

This knitted sweater, one of de Kort's extreme miniatures, is so small it fits on the head of a pin. It's fashioned from the sort of Egyptian cotton thread that's usually reserved for embroidery. *Photo by Annelies de Kort*

strongest reading glasses and looked through my magnifying glass. And no matter how small it is," claims de Kort, "I often like to try a little knitting in stripes."

As if this weren't extreme enough, de Kort proceeded to take the step beyond a step beyond. Lying in a wee flower garden tableau is a doll so small you have to squint to see it. It's wearing a little seafoam and pink number knitted by de Kort in 1:160 scale. *How?*

"I can do this micro-knitting only for a short time in the morning, when my eyes and I are still fresh," offers de Kort, who uses needles ranging from Dutch number 20/0.8mm to number 26/0.4mm. "And I have noticed that I hold my breath while I make the stitches."

More of de Kort's microknit sweaters. *Photo by Annelies de Kort*

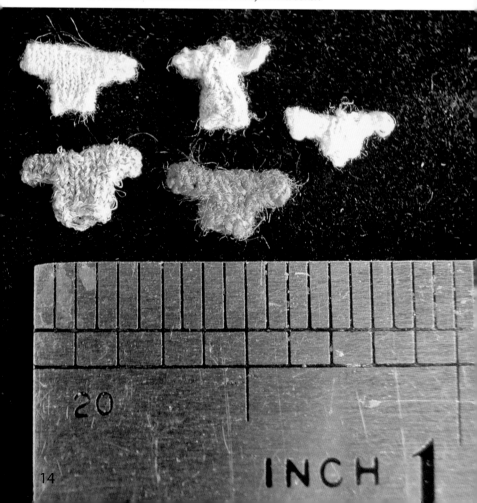

Knitting Big and Long

This is knitting that could cover your whole town. And some of it does.

PYRAMID PIECE

ANDY HOLDEN

A Rock That's Almost as Big as a Pyramid!

Most visitors to Giza, Egypt, buy postcards of the pyramids as souvenirs. Brit Andy Holden, age twelve, took a piece of an actual pyramid—a small nugget of rock that had chipped off the pyramid Cheops. Perhaps an inordinate amount of guilt about this "theft" ensued until, consumed with remorse and the beginnings of an idea for an art piece, Holden returned to Egypt to return the rock some fifteen years later. Then, he went about re-creating the piece of rock. In yarn. At a size 100,000 times that of the original.

Using models and diagrams as a reference, Holden knitted *Pyramid Piece* out of more wool than he could be bothered to tally up, for a stunningly large surface area of about 592 square feet (55 square meters). "I was hoping to make a monument to a monument," explains Holden of the faux-rock's extreme size. Also, it was "meant to be a representation of how the stone *seemed* to me as a child—which was much bigger than it really was, as my guilt from having taken it mutated into a larger presence. It's common for objects encountered as a child to seem bigger than they are, and when the objects are revisited as an adult they seem smaller. And it's not just because our bodies have changed in size, but for psychological reasons also."

Andy Holden's enormous oeuvre, *Pyramid Piece*, seen from every angle. The knitted piece is one hundred times larger than the original bit of limestone Holden snagged from Giza during a boyhood trip. Knitted yarns, foam, steel support, 9½ feet × 13 feet × 16½ feet (3m × 4m × 5m). *Photos courtesy of the artist*

All that having been said, what is a further curiosity about this rock-writ-large is its spooky similarity to the original—although Holden claims the colors are exaggerated, like "colors of a cartoon." To achieve the overall effect, Holden and his assistant experimented with wool to develop new ways of achieving textures and colors. For example, says the artist, "we would cut tiny bits of yarn up and then tie them onto a cone of yarn to get flecks and speckles of color. We also broke several chunky knitting machines by trying to feed up to fourteen yarns through at one time, often with a couple of DKs and ten two-ply yarns. In the end, it was more like painting—constantly mixing colors to get the desired look."

The knitted skin was stretched over foam, and a metal frame constructed of bent mattress needles and wire that was designed to "allow the shape to be enlarged and retain the feel of the shape of the original piece." The result? A giant sculpture as soft as a child's toy. The biggest toy you ever saw.

"I was hoping to make a monument to a monument," explains Holden of the faux-rock's extreme size.

PHAT KNITS

BAUKE KNOTTNERUS

Fat, Too!

They're big threads. *Really* big, foam-filled threads. And they've been equated with everything from "Spaghetti Monsterism" to portals to a *Honey, I Shrunk the Kids* experience. They're "Phat Knits" by twenty-five-year-old Rotterdam artist Bauke Knottnerus, used to knit up massive seats and carpets you can then scatter around your (presumably also massive) home.

While the threads themselves are industrially manufactured, the actual knitting of them must be done by hand—as many as four pairs of hands, wielding 13-foot PVC needles. Says Knottnerus of his somewhat amorphous-resulting creations, "It starts with a joke, but after that it could be anything."

Yes, really phat, fat anythings.

Overzicht2, Phat Knits 2 Just some of the knits you can create with Knottnerus' Phat Knits. *Photos courtesy of Bauke Knottnerus. Phat Knits 2008*

5
THE KNITTING MACHINE

DAVE COLE

Macho Machine-Made Material!

It's difficult to say who Providence, Rhode Island, sculptor Dave Cole's biggest fans are: die-hard knitting enthusiasts bowled over by his unconventional crafting techniques, or grizzled gearheads who just want to sidle up to his tools. To illustrate this point, Cole tells a story about the latter: a couple of visitors to the 2005 installation of his *Knitting Machine* exhibit at the MASS MoCA contemporary art center in North Adams, Massachusetts.

"An old-timer showed up while we were setting up the day before," recalls Cole. "He had been a career excavator operator for forty years, and he wanted to see what was going on. He came back the next day with his grandson. They brought folding chairs and watched for eight hours, fascinated. It was quality time for the two of them."

The objects of their fascination were pretty plainly fascinating: two John Deere excavators wielding utility poles to knit a mile of felt into an American flag that measured, when complete, 20 feet high and 30 feet wide. In the center of it all, standing in a cherry picker, was Cole, wielding a gaff—the sort of hook used by fishermen to pull large sea critters aboard—to help pass the "yarn" over the "needles."

"Basically," muses Cole, "I was the pinky. But I didn't want to stick my hands into the heavy equipment."

To orchestrate such an event was no mean feat. It was nine months in the planning, during which time Cole created scale models—not only of the flag but of the excavators, too; figured out the gauge for the scale and how many stitches he'd be able to use per row; fabricated tips for the two utility poles out of wood and figured out how to attach them; got himself and three friends licensed as excavator operators; then taught those friends, quite literally, how to knit with yarn and conventional needles.

It made perfect sense for them to do this, he says. "An excavator is just an extension of an arm, so once they figured out how they needed their hands to work, they could do it on a bigger scale."

Cole chose to use felt as his knitting material because it's "lightweight, doesn't hold water; it's colorfast and strong." But other than that, "It's the same regular felt you buy in squares in a craft store, only the manufacturing company cut custom rolls for me into strips two feet wide."

In fact, Cole had a lot of help in creating the *Knitting Machine*, and one could argue that the level of community involvement paralleled, if not rivaled, conventional knitting circles and bees. Custom-cut felt. Brand-new excavators borrowed from a local equipment supply store. Utility pole attachments manufactured by another local enterprise. Friends working the excavators. And of course, the admiring support of retired excavator operators, their grandsons, and hundreds of knitting and gear enthusiasts who gathered together to watch the monumental unfurling.

Dave Cole's *Knitting Machine* stitches up a flag at MASS MoCA. *Photo courtesy of theknittingmachine.com and Judi Rotenberg Gallery, Boston, Mass.*

HASE

GELITIN

Appearance of Big Bunny Bowls Over Populace!

One morning in 2005, suddenly, there it was: an enormous pink rabbit, 200 feet long and 20 feet high, splayed across the mountainous landscape of Artesina, Italy, as though dropped en route to delivery by an enormous stork. The arrival of this bunny at an altitude of 5,000 feet, however, was no accident. It was carefully planned and orchestrated by those darlings of the contemporary art world, Vienna-based collective gelitin, known for its whimsical and delightful stagings. The rabbit was five years in the knitting, by "dozens of grannies" out of pink wool, according to the group. In the end, quips Ali Janka, one of four gelitins, "The grannies were aided by a knitting machine, because the people got tired after knitting an arm and a leg."

> "Knitting is a time-string folded back on itself over and over again."

Janka somewhat deliriously maintains that the rabbit is constructed of "a ton" of synthetic and wool yarn, the purchase of which was "triggered by a certain mood in the morning." Models were made, and from the models a pattern was constructed, although Janka, ever cagey in his answers, is sketchy on details. He will admit to a number of technical challenges, however: getting all the materials up the mountain, managing the huge amount of straw used to stuff the rabbit, and figuring out how to "fix" the straw so that it would not slide down the slope, as the rabbit lies on an incline.

Special permission was granted to gelitin by the owner of the land, and the county in which the land resides, to erect the rabbit. Asserts Janka, "This was the best spot—it's in the mountains, and you have to walk up to see it. You can walk on higher mountains and look down upon it. At the same time, it is embedded in a landscape that is used for skiing slopes with steel and concrete buildings rising out of the mountainsides. The landscape is beautifully rotting, and so is the rabbit." It will remain at its site (now designated "Rabbit Hill") for twenty years, subjecting itself to the rigors of the elements and the tramplings of spectators.

As for the inspiration behind the rabbit, one can consult the group's press materials for a semblance of an answer: "Happily in love you step down the decaying corpse, through the wound, now small like a maggot, over woolen kidney and bowel. Happy you leave like the larva that gets its wings from an innocent carcass at the roadside. Such is the happiness which made this rabbit. I love the rabbit the rabbit loves me."

Or consider Janka's explanation of the matter: "Knitting is a time-string folded back on itself over and over again.

The first and only rabbit ever to be viewable from space. Here, witnessed a little closer to Earth, from the window of an airplane. *gelitin, Rabbit, Artesina, Piemont, Italy, 2005–2025, Photo © gelitin*

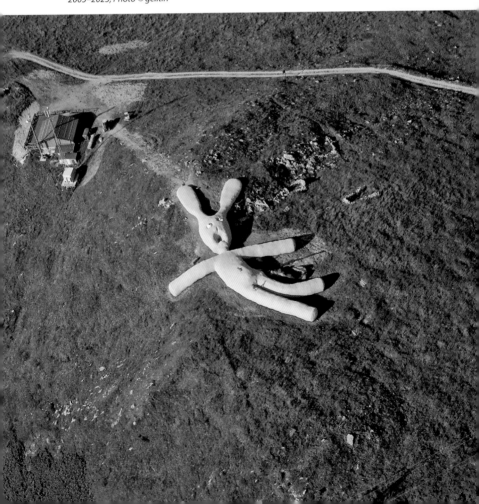

Also, the rabbit refers to all the small knitted animals that are made by hand for children and get more love-hours than can ever be repaid."

Clear this "explanation" may not be, except in this one consideration: The vision of a gargantuan pink rabbit lolling between mountains is sure to elicit cries of wonder and amazement from children, and everyone else who sees it. Which may very well be explanation enough. As is this: The rabbit is possibly the first-ever piece of knitting to be visible from space.

The rapidly decomposing rabbit, still soft enough to snooze on for those intent upon a nap. *Photo © gelitin*

THE KNITTED MILE

ROBYN LOVE

All Around a Texas Town!

Seeking to offer up an alternative to a culture (namely, the city of Dallas, Texas) where "the car is king," Robyn Love unfurled her *Knitted Mile* project one chilly morning in February 2008. Garter-stitched using four hundred skeins of donated Lion Brand Yarn *Vanna's Choice* acrylic in gold, this installation would, when completely exhibited, snake down the center of Hill Street from Main Street to North Haskell, looking very much like a painted center line.

"In a car, the landscape is seen and experienced at seventy miles per hour," explains Love as she talks about her 4-inch-wide slither of yellow. "When you knit, the yarn is experienced stitch by stitch, inch by inch. I wanted to juxtapose these two diametrically opposed experiences, lay one on top of the other, as a way of causing a moment of interruption to our seventy-mile-per-hour lives."

The piece also caused interruptions of another kind. As Love was just beginning to unravel the strip "like a fire hose," as she describes it, "an SUV stopped and asked what we were

The Knitted Mile piled in back of the car. *Photo by Shannon Stratton*

up to. But when I told them it was art, they drove away."
A bit later, a truck driver who had watched the goings-on
orchestrated by Love and two assistants very politely rolled
down his window and asked permission to cross. The stripe
looked so convincing, cars followed it precisely, even when it
swerved and jogged. "One car even nearly ran off the road in
order to follow the line," Love recalls.

Perhaps luckily for early morning Dallas drivers, the
stripe, which was created by about ninety knitters and was
arduous both to stitch and to lay out, wound up being
somewhat less than a mile: 0.36 of a mile, to be precise.
But "it sure looked convincing."

Well, it wasn't quite a mile, but it sure was long! From top,
clockwise: Love begins the unfurling, the looooong view,
and a close-up. *Photos by Shannon Stratton*

THE KNITTED RIVER

I KNIT

Long May It Ripple!

It may have been the largest knitted project ever undertaken: nearly 100,000 squares huge, using countless yards of yarn, all as part of a 2007 campaign to raise awareness of the 1.1 billion people worldwide who do not have access to safe drinking water. With *The Knitted River*, a collaboration between a charity called WaterAid, owners of the London shop I Knit, and thousands of craftspeople around the world, seeing the project in all its watery splendor was definitely believing.

The Knitted River, draped over the roof of London's National Theatre on July 14, 2006. *Photo courtesy of I Knit*

BIGSOCK

JOANNA RATCLIFFE

Sock for a Giant Travels the World!

Bigsock, a contender for the world's biggest sock record, started its life on the planet as a plain old circular knit sock. It was meant simply to raise money for the Sara Lee Trust, a UK charity that provides alternate therapies to people who are terminally ill, according to *Bigsock's* organizer, Joanna Ratcliffe. But then it grew. And grew.

Since its worthy but humble origins, knitters have been clubbing together to keep the sock moving around the world, and to cover the postage for moving it. It travels with a log, a record signed by everyone who has ever knitted on it. "This, with all the photos and the blog, act as proof enough of what we have achieved in order to surpass the current Guinness record for Biggest Sock," says Ratcliffe. That record was established in March 2008 by an Austrian sheep farmer's association called Schafhaltervereinigung Inn-Hausruckvientel (try saying that ten times fast), and it measured 16 feet 3 inches by 14 feet 1 inch by 6 feet 2 inches.

Reports Ratcliffe, "Ours is much bigger, and considering the work that has gone into it, I would think it will be a hard one to beat. *Bigsock* will also need to be validated when it is finished

The *Bigsock*, in progress. *Photo by Terri L. Randolph, Larkspur Studio*

by two experts. Not sure if it will set any other records, although one of the obvious ones is Most Knitters to Have Worked on a Single Object." At press time, the sock was a little over 13 feet long, with Ratcliffe preparing to send the work to Germany, where the toe was to be cast on.

Around the House

People have long knit knickknacks to gussy up the house. These crafters have actually knit the house. And everything in it.

THE KNITTED GINGERBREAD HOUSE

ALISON MURRAY

Ewe'll Be Home for Christmas!

How do you best an ornately decorated Christmas gingerbread house? Knit it instead of baking it and bedecking it with colorful candy. Knit it in life size. Knit not only its outside, but its insides, too: tables, chairs, stove, plants, curtains, cuckoo clock, and an entire sumptuous tea party.

Just such a house was conceived in 2007 by forty-five-year-old Alison Murray of Devon, England. Obviously, a project of this magnitude presented far too much knitting for Murray alone, and, in the end, she managed to solicit the help of about five hundred knitters from around the globe to work on *The Knitted Gingerbread House*, which raised some £24,000 for

the Great Ormond Street Hospital for Children and North Devon Hospice, two of Murray's pet charities.

Patterns were sent around for sweets (like the gingerbread men pattern included in this book) and cakes; knitters were also asked to knit up 10-inch squares to construct the roof and walls—which were supported by a metal frame—as well as "anything they thought would suit the house and garden," explains Murray. The house was on display for several months in a local shopping mall and was seen by an estimated 423,000 visitors.

Murray herself stitched up a cuckoo clock, a fire extinguisher, and a box of matches to stash inside the 140-square-foot house. Other contributions included a sideboard; a dresser;

Knit your own Gingerbread Man with the pattern on page 227!

Baker's pride: the completed *Knitted Gingerbread House*, as seen from the outside … and looking in, at the amazing assemblage of knitted furniture, rugs, treats, and embellishments. *Photos courtesy of Alison Murray*

Above: A hand-knit tea party. Below: The *Knitted Gingerbread House* bedroom is especially cozy. *Photos courtesy of Alison Murray*

a bed; 12-foot trees, some festooned with fungi; primroses, daisies, and ivy for the garden; pictures, including a "home sweet home" sampler and a portrait of a girl; a lace tablecloth complete with a full English breakfast of bacon, eggs, sausages, mushrooms, black pudding, and a fried egg; and hundreds of gingerbread men. It all looked delicious enough to eat—especially, one would reasonably assume, if you were a giant moth.

11

KEUKEN 2007 AND BADKAMER

DÉSIRÉE DE BAAR

Fixtures You Can Snuggle Up To!

Dutch artist Désirée de Baar learned to knit from her mother when she was about eight years old. Little did her family suspect then that she would go on to use this homey craft to create sleek sculptures of some of the most banal home utilities in existence: a kitchen sink and a bathtub.

"There are different things to say about how [knitting] suits the pieces," says de Baar. "There's the contradiction between the subject and the material, the hard and the soft. … Unusual and unexpected, which makes you look better at ordinary things. The intensity of making gives an extra value to the subject, which is often an ordinary thing. Small details become poetic."

De Baar's knitted sculptures straddle the line between realistic

De Baar's life-size *Badkamer*, replete with fixtures and soap dish. *Photos courtesy of RAM, Rotterdam, photos by Désirée de Baar*

and interpretive. They are life-size copies and painstakingly measured, and yet, they are exhibited with de Baar's sketches—in the kitchen, hot pink faucets are attached to the wall atop grids representing tiles and outlines for pipes; in the bathroom, a soap dish and faucet are pinned to the wall over sketches of themselves. This only draws closer attention to the fact that they are made of knitting. De Baar's may be the only bathtub in existence that anyone would actually want to curl up and sleep in.

Says de Baar, "I like the mathematical aspect of the knitting and the way that affects my subjects. I transform or re-create them by processing all the steps. A close observation is the first step [in making the work]." For the bathtub, de Baar drew lines on an actual tub to divide it into measurable parts. She measured all those lines and created a paper model. In this way, she was able to calculate patterns for stitches. The dimensions are all at actual size. *Keuken* 2007 is about 8 feet wide and 19 inches deep.

"I always aim for the lightest construction," de Baar explains. "On the other hand, I don't want the works to collapse or lose shape. So, for the bathtub I used wooden sticks [to hold it up]. And for the pink kitchen sink, I made a steel construction that consisted only of bars under the seams—just a skeleton.

"Everybody wants to touch these works," exclaims de Baar. "The material—100 percent wool—attracts, and people want to find out how the piece was constructed. So they push the surface to see if it is soft or stuffed. And I hope that people will look with a renewed eye at casual things. Maybe slow down a little and take a closer look."

Keuken, 2007. *Keuken's* pink kitchen sink and close-up of faucet. *Photos courtesy of RAM, Rotterdam, photos by Désirée de Baar and Joep Vogels, Audax Textielmuseum*

12
YURT

KATE POKORNY
Warmer Than an Igloo!

Where Jan Messent (see page 108) taught a generation of knitters how to make castles for dolls, Kate Pokorny means to crochet yurts—well, at least one yurt to start—for full-size humans. In so doing, she's had to kick up her usual crafting scale by an increment or ten. She's using 500 pounds of unscoured, felted, donated New Hampshire wool and her own arm as a crochet hook. "I had initially whittled a huge hook," Pokorny says, "but it didn't afford me the flexibility I needed to grab the felted cording and pull it back through." She's aiming for a final construction measuring 10 feet by 10 feet.

"The most important piece of the pattern was to increase stitches at a regular pace so things didn't get out of whack," explains Pokorny. Needless to say, this work has not been all smooth sailing. "The biggest challenge was the actual

Pokorny's sketch for her soon-to-be-yurt. *Illustration by Thyra Heder*

crocheting—I really had to wrestle that cording! What I learned from the prototype was that if I'm going to put the cording in the washing machine to further the felting, I only need to do one cycle. Two made it way too dense." There was also the all-important matter of flipping the yurt, which Pokorny crocheted "from the oculus and working up and out, right side up"—no simple task.

Sadly, Pokorny has no immediate plans to live in her yurt, although who knows? "My dream would be to cover it in a solar-luminescent fabric, which could be made into a cover that would harvest the sun's energy to power internal lights," she muses. "Yes, that would be my dream."

Swatching. *Photo by Kate Pokorny*

13
WILLOW PATTERN CUP AND LIDDED WEDGEWOOD BOX

DEBBIE NEW

China You Can't Eat Off!

Tucked into the pages of Debbie New's 2003 Schoolhouse Press title, *Unexpected Knitting*, was a pattern for a piece that may have seemed, on first consideration, to be "unexpected" due mostly to its mundanity. What's so amazing about knitting a teacup? Well, in this instance, pretty much everything, including the explanation for its existence and, particularly, how it came to be constructed.

Says New: "Early in my knitting explorations, I attended a presentation by Rachel McHenry on her wonderful knitted hats, which inspired me to try some. Knitted hats are sculptures with minds of their own about the shape they want to be. So I wanted to try something freestanding that could hold its shape without stiffener." To achieve this, New knitted her cup in the shape of a football, then tucked one end of it into the other. "One half is in stranded knitting, and the other is in stocking stitch with a purl row between to sharpen

New's *Willow Pattern Cup* looks as pretty as real china. *Photo by Janet New*

the fold line," she explains. "The double layer provides extra strength as the natural curl of the two sides is in opposition." Now, why didn't you think of that?

New's *Lidded Wedgewood Box* takes a similarly unremarkable base concept—a knitted toilet roll cover, in this instance meant for inclusion in Lucy Neatby's 1998 exhibit of such items—and propels it into the extraordinary. "I challenged myself to knit all the decoration without sewing on any of the additional lines," says New. "Most of it was worked in stranded knitting with traveling stitches and some texture. Since there were places where single threads were called for, one half of a long stitch sometimes wandered up the visible side with the other half hidden for a few rounds."

Debbie New proves, as she has so often in her career, that great ideas become truly brilliant in the making of them. Well, in *her* making of them.

Lidded Wedgewood Box was designed as a toilet paper roll cover. *Photo by Janet New*

All Around Town

We've already knit the house. Why stop there? These knitters saw no reason why they shouldn't move on to larger environments.

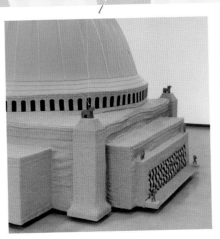

14
KNITTED BUILDINGS

ANNETTE STREYL

All the Makings of a Lifelike Miniature City!

Hamburg-based Annette Streyl is a widely acclaimed visual artist whose architectural sculptures rely on two disparate and, some would argue, contradictory materials to give them form. One is stone. The other is wool, which she machine-knits into gorgeous, pliant, and also highly recognizable and politically loaded structures: a McDonald's, an IKEA, New York's AT&T building (now known as the Sony Tower), and, perhaps most

famously, the Berlin Reichstag, the original of which caught fire under mysterious circumstances during the time of the Third Reich. No one who's seen the originals could possibly mistake the woolly copies for anything other than what they're meant to represent. They're just a tad … *woollier*.

Streyl shows them stretched over their armatures, where their true and recognizable structures are immediately apparent, and also without, strung over lines as though they were billows of strange, useless clothing. "Both versions of my sculptures have the same importance and are exhibited equally," says Streyl. "With the armature, you can compare the size (as it's all done to a scale of 1:100) and the shape of the

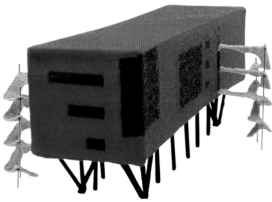

buildings. The version without armature is more ironic and fits better the soft material of wool (which doesn't like to be at an angle). This version is my personal favorite. As every building has or is a logo, the viewer can still recognize it."

Streyl says that materials are especially important in achieving just the right look for her buildings—yarn color in particular, "which must fit to the color of the building." She uses Lurex to represent glass façades. Meanwhile, her architectural structures are prone to the same kinds of catastrophes that plague your average sweater knitter. Says Streyl, "I try not to use pure wool, because of the moths."

A version of this entry first appeared in *Twist Collective* Winter 2010. Visit twistcollective.com.

Streyl's amazing knitted buildings: left to right, New York City's AT&T building (now the Sony Tower), one of Berlin's ubiquitous "Info" boxes; and the Great Hall (with and without armature). *Photos of the Great Hall and AT&T building, Ulrich Gehner; photo of Info-Box, Alexander Rischer*

KNITTED HOMES OF CRIME

FREDDIE ROBINS

Tea-Cozy Murder Sites!

In 2002, Brighton, England, native Freddie Robins was commissioned by the Firstsight gallery in Colchester to make an unusual series of works: tea cozies in the shape of houses. Not just any houses, mind you, but houses where crimes (in all cases, murders) occurred, or where a criminal (in all cases, the subjects were murderesses) lived.

Robins set to work investigating historic homicides throughout England and hit upon seven riveting candidates: Christiana Edmunds, a notorious poisoner; Mrs. Beard, the woman Edmunds tried to poison (her lethal chocolates

found their way into the hands—and stomach—of four-year-old Sidney Barker instead); Mary Eleanor Wheeler, who in 1890 slit the throat of her lover's wife and also killed his daughter; Ethel Major, who poisoned her husband with strychnine; Charlotte Bryant, who poisoned her husband with arsenic; Styllou Christofi, hanged in 1954 for murdering her daughter-in-law (it's possible she also murdered her mother-in-law); and Ruth Ellis, who shot her race-car-driver lover in 1955.

Despite, or perhaps because of, the grisly nature of the subject matter, Robins calls *Knitted Homes of Crime* her "favorite piece of work."

It's cozy knitting that's about as far from "cozy" as you can possibly get. Crumpet, anyone?

A view of Robins' installation of *Knitted Homes of Crime*, 2002 (wool, quilted lining fabric). *Photo by Douglas Atfield, knitting by Jean Arkell*

FREDDIE ROBINS

IN HER OWN WORDS

The knitted tea cozy in the form of a twee knitted country cottage can often be found. I have a few in my own collection. I also have quite a few patterns for them. I had always thought what hideous, cloying, claustrophobic objects they were and what an undesirable, claustrophobic way of life they represented.

At the same time, I had always wanted to make a piece of work that discussed female killers—I had quite a lot of publications about this subject. These ideas became linked, and I did further research to find the kinds of crimes that I was interested in.

In some cases, I found images of the houses in books. In some cases, the houses no longer existed, and I used local historians to figure out how the houses looked. I went to look at all the houses or sites of houses in London (where I lived at the time) and in Brighton (where I grew up and my parents still live), and photographed them. I did not use very recent cases, as I didn't want the work to be sensational or sensationalized. And I was only interested in female killers who acted alone. Women are always doubly dammed for crime, in particular murder: once for the crime, and then once again for going against what we believe is the female nature of caring and nurturing. I loved this little rhyme that I discovered during my research, "When poison is found, the murderer's gowned."

Much of my work is about subversion: subversion of ideas, processes, and objects. I am particularly interested in the undervalued, underappreciated, and overlooked. We supposedly live in a time of sexual equality, but all around me I see glaring evidence of gross inequality. Here were women killing, and often through an act that we perceive as being an act of love: cooking. The contrast between these sweet, knitted houses and the gross acts of violence committed within them or by the women who occupied them is very powerful.

The houses are all knitted in basic double knitting yarn. I translated images into knitting patterns in the form of knitting diagrams, using symbols to indicate the different colors and stitches to be used. The diagrams were littered with notes and little stitch samples for my friend Julie's mother, Jean Arkell, to knit—I also sent her photographs and the stories behind the murders. She is an excellent hand-knitter and likes a challenge.

We worked on one house per month. Whilst Jean was knitting one house, I was preparing the pattern for the next. The houses were knitted in pieces with separate sections for the front, back, sides, chimneys, etc. Jean sent the pieces back to me, and I embroidered on the detail, sewed them up, and lined them. There are seven houses in all: Charlotte, Christiana, Eleanor, Ethel, Mrs. Beard, Ruth, and Styllou. They are constructed as actual tea cozies that could be put over a teapot. They are lined with white quilted cotton fabric. When they are shown, I simply stuff them with tissue paper so that they can stand up.

Included with the information that accompanies the houses when they are exhibited is the number of hours that it took to knit the pieces. I included them because I liked the way that, when Jean returned the knitted pieces, she wrote them down so that I could pay her fairly for the work done. I thought this information juxtaposed well with the other information provided. It is a reminder of the time women spent, and still do spend, on completely overlooked, undervalued, yet necessary domestic tasks, and contrasts well with the unknown time taken to kill. How long did these women take to kill? Were they planning for years, months, days, or were they spontaneous acts?

Robins and the sweet, woolly house of a vicious murderess. *Photo by Peter Sharpe, knitting by Jean Arkell*

I don't have a favorite murder, but I do have a favorite house. The ugly little semi-detached Ethel. If I were made to live there, I would kill, too, but probably myself.

16

RE-IMAGINING THE CENTRE— YARN BOMBINGS

Keeping the Dead Warm!

Yarn bombing's everywhere you look these days—on lampposts, on buses (see page 88), and on parking meters, probably in a town near you. It's largely unsanctioned, and harmless enough to make the average viewer wonder what all the fuss is about. Why is it illegal in Sweden, for example? And why did people in an Ohio town recently get their knickers in a twist about a sweater for a tree (find out on page 133)?

The Sundogs cozies covered two of the oldest gravestones behind the oldest church in Inverness. This was the execution site of Jacobite prisoners after the battle of Culloden in 1745—bullet marks riddle some of the gravestones. *Photo by Ewen Weatherspoon, artwork by Sundogs*

The yarn bombing by the Sundogs for the occasion of Inverness, Scotland's "Re-Imagining the Centre" event in 2009 was yarn bombing of a slightly different stripe, however. First, it was commissioned by the event's organizers as part of a push to "Give folk permission to claim back the public spaces as places for people and the things that people want to do," according to curator Matt Baker.

The Sundogs used almost 28 miles (45 kilometers) of red acrylic yarn to knit three "dancing dresses" that flew over a popular pub, a series of arrows leading all through the streets, and

46

cobwebs (actually, these were crocheted) stretching across a tucked-away courtyard. But it was their three gravestone covers that generated the most press, and a lot of sniping. In newspaper accounts, critics said the cozies were "in bad taste," and "disrespectful ... no matter how old [the gravestones] are."

Countered Annie Marrs and Jen Cantwell, the two artists who make up Sundogs, and who spent several months fighting an ancient knitting machine in order to churn out the cozy pieces, "We don't see it as offensive. We see it as a humorous, noninvasive interaction with our environment. Yarn bombing ... throws up issues of ownership and boundaries. Who exactly owns public space? We do—we *are* the public."

The words *coorie in* are knitted into the largest of the three cozies. Says Jen Cantwell, "This Scots term means to snuggle in, to cuddle. It's one of those words that doesn't get justice in translation because it's as much an emotion as it is words." *Photo by Ewen Weatherspoon, artwork by Sundogs*

VISIONS OF OLD VINCENNES AFGHAN

JANE CAMPBELL

A Whole Town in One Blanket!

Seeking to honor her hometown of Vincennes, Indiana, in 2004, needlework fanatic Jane Campbell set out to stitch its history into an afghan. "I love telling stories through texture," claims Campbell, who's been knitting for more than fifty years.

Plumbing the depths of her extensive stitch dictionary library, Campbell worked out a group of patterns to represent

Campbell knit her whole town's history into one pattern-stitch blanket. *Photo by Jane Campbell*

some of the most iconic of the town's landmarks and details: Cathedral, Arched Windows, Small Bricks, and two of her own devising for a central panel representing St. Francis Xavier Church; Bricks and Willow Buds for Grouseland, the town's first brick structure and once the home of ninth president William Henry Harrison; Hunters Stitch for the town's trapper ancestors; and Arrowheads for the Piankeshaw tribe, the original inhabitants of the region.

"Many, many hours are spent working out the details of a design, so by the time that's finished, I can't wait to knit it and move on to the next project," says Campbell, who used Lion Brand Yarn *Wool-Ease Chunky* and size 10½ needles for the original afghan—there are now two extant afghans, and a third on the way.

Unfortunately, "what seems plausible on paper isn't always perfect in practice. Of course, I learned that the hard way and made many trips to the frog pond." Wonder where that would fit on Campbell's blanket?

THE KNITTED VILLAGE

A Village for Ants!

It took forty ladies (give or take a lady) thousands of hours to knit this village, which may be comparable to the amount of time it took masons and architects to build the real thing in life size out of bricks and mortar.

It all began more than two decades ago with a quest to save a single building—the Mersham Town Hall in Mersham, UK, which in 1986 had fallen on hard times. Going door to door, Mersham's original band of twelve Afternoon Club ladies offered to knit replicas of people's homes in exchange for a donation to save the hall. Size and scale mattered; the late husband of one of the ladies took photos and measurements all around town, then created three-dimensional cardboard templates for the knitters to work from. By the time the village was completed, a few ladies—most of whom today are firmly entrenched in their eighties—had, let's say, *passed on* to other things. And sixty properties in all had been knitted. Among them are several dozen houses, some with thatched roofs and hedgerows, or with cars in the driveway, or with chickens in the yard; the Norman-era church, replete with gravestones; a telephone box; a wheelbarrow; a bus shelter; a cricket pitch and cricketers; two pubs; the school; and the once-doomed town hall, on whose behalf £10,000 was raised when the club first exhibited their creation around the county.

Afterward, with the town hall saved to exist another day, the mini-village was packed away and forgotten. Then, in 2007, the Afternoon Club retrieved it from storage and began to sell off its pieces, once again in the interest of putting money into the coffers of the hall. Sad though the ladies may have been to break up the tableau, there was a happy side to the sale: Owners of most of the real homes walked away with the tiny knitted doppelgangers.

Transportation

How do you—or your knits—get around a knitted town? In, on, or through some sort of knitted vehicle, of course.

19

FERRARI

LAUREN PORTER

Knot-Wheels!

Wondering what to do with ten months of your time and 12 miles of yarn? How about knitting a car? How about knitting the car to end all cars—a Ferrari Testarossa with a bit of the F355 thrown in for good measure? That's precisely what Lauren Porter did in 2006, when it came time to produce a senior project to gain her sculpture degree at Bath Spa University in England. She thought it would be "instantly recognizable." And has it ever been.

"The first reactions to the Ferrari were a bit of a frenzy," recalls Porter. "The local papers took pictures of it, and then the next day it was in every single British tabloid. It was very exciting and positive; whole ranges of people responded to it—kids, men, women, car fanatics, and knitters. It was great!"

The adulation came only after countless hours of serious hard work—both by Porter and the group of friends and family who assisted her in knitting the 250 squares and

Porter's 100 percent wool Ferrari, stitched from a boggling 12 miles of yarn. *Photo by Tricia Porter*

rectangles from Sirdar *Bonus Chunky* yarn to form the body of the superlative vehicle. "The whole project was a huge challenge!" Porter says. "I built the frame first, scaling it up from a toy car. I wanted to make it so that it would fold down, but to look like it was one solid object when assembled. I also wanted it to look as much like a car as possible without caricaturing it too much." Knitting, says Porter, was actually the perfect medium for the task: "It's such a constructive, sculptural process, and very portable, so it can be done in the pub or on the bus, not just in the studio," she explains.

"The first reactions to the Ferrari were a bit of a frenzy," recalls Porter. "The local papers took pictures of it, and then the next day it was in every single British tabloid."

Although the car is now in storage, it had a good run of viewings—in Paris, all over England, and perhaps most fittingly, at the British Motor Show, where it was housed in a super car paddock alongside a row of real Ferraris. "The company must have seen it in the press!" exclaims Porter, although she hasn't heard a word of response from them.

But consider this: BMW boasts a prototype with a fabric skin. Could a fully functioning knitted race car be far behind?

20

MOTORCYCLE COZY

THERESA HONEYWELL

If Your Motorcycle Could Talk, This Is What It Would Ask For!

No, Theresa Honeywell won't be jumping aboard this pretty Kawasaki Z650 and taking it for a spin anytime soon. For starters, "It has no carburetor." Also, what with the hundreds of knitted cozies swaddling each of its still-remaining parts, the engine "would burn it up to pieces," she asserts.

Which would be a pity, after all the attention Honeywell has lavished on it. First off, she rescued the motorcycle from the junk heap in the town of Anderson, South Carolina. "I saw these great bikes just piled up and rotting away," she recalls. "They were empowering symbols that were once so important and had been discarded." She felt the same way about her marriage. "I was married quite young and it was all wrong," she explains, and through the motorcycle, she decided to express her feelings of powerlessness and attempt to counteract them. "I wanted more out of life. I covered the

A cozy for a motorcycle, Honeywell-style, on display at the Everything Nice Georgia show. For more information on the work of Theresa Honeywell please visit Theresahoneywell.com.

bike as a symbol; the pink yarn softens the rusty masculine metal and embraces it."

In transforming the motorcycle, Honeywell went through about twenty-five skeins of Red Heart acrylic ("I love handmade yarns, but cheap granny-style yarn was most appropriate for this") in pretty much every shade of raspberry, baby pink, white, and mauve she could find at

For gearheads, a close-up of the engine.

the yarn shop. Each little bit of the bike was covered, from the spark plugs to the brake cables. "I used fans and feathers to cover the tires—they mimicked the tread; lots of cables, lace, and ribbing. I tried to replicate or emphasize what was beneath," says Honeywell.

Perhaps this cozy's biggest fans: "Big, burly biker guys love it!" she marvels. "They find it fascinating that I've paid so much respect to something that they love and relate to."

21

WIND KNITTING FACTORY

MEREL KARHOF

Knits Scarves Using Real Wind!

Nonknitters, here's something for you—a machine that can make a scarf without you! But if the idea of a knitting machine sounds a bit familiar, well … this one assuredly isn't. *Wind Knitting Factory*, designed and built as a thesis project by then–master's student Merel Karhof using parts from a 1900 Wikuna sock machine, harnesses the gusty effects of Mother Nature to achieve its yarny purpose. To wit: yard upon yard of scarf churned out, sometimes fast, sometimes slow, depending on the whim of the wind, along the rooftop of an apartment building in London's South Kensington neighborhood, where Karhof first set it in motion.

Funnily enough, Karhof, who is not a knitter herself, found inspiration in a dead end. "While I was trying to walk from the Royal College of Art towards Kensington, I was confronted with lots of cul-de-sacs," she says. "Interesting to me was the way the wind blows in and out of these spaces, unlike normal streets, where the wind blows only in one

Karhof's knitting machine in place, harnessing the wind for the good of knitting.

Wind Knitting Factory, as seen from above. *Wind Knitting Factory by Merel Karhof*

55

direction." She decided to make something of it. After whipping up a series of models for a few of the possibilities that popped to mind—wind-powered drawing machine, wind-powered telephone—she hit upon this happy concept, although she found it was a grand challenge to make the wheel perfectly round, make the blades perfectly alike, and keep the yarn—Italian cashwool—on the machine. "But I think all knitters know that problem," Karhof quips.

As of this writing, the machine had made about twenty-five scarves. The never-ending tube gets "harvested" from time to time, and lengths of it cut into 6½-foot (2-meter) sections that are labeled with the date they were made, as well as the amount of time it took for the machine to knit them. The fastest knits so far? Three blue scarves (totaling about 20 feet of knitting) in eight hours.

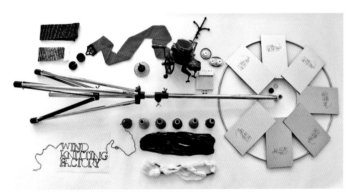

The components: Everything you need to make your own Wind Knitting Factory (not seen in this photo: the wind).

A sampling of scarves knit using the wind knitting machine.

Good Enough to Eat ... and Food for Thought

These knits aren't delicious (unless you are a member of the order Lepidoptera). But they sure do make the mouth water!

22

KNITTED SEDER

"KNITTIVIST" LESLIE SUDOCK

Just in Time for the High Holy Days!

Since 2007, Leslie Sudock has been concocting a giant feast. This one won't make you feel bloated from overeating, though, only cause a slight, empathetic ache in the fingers as you contemplate the rigors of its creation. For the *Knitted Seder* is, of course, entirely knitted.

First up, there are all the usual components of the Seder plate:

Beitzah (roasted egg) — a symbol of mourning for the destruction of the Temple in Jerusalem

Zeroah (roasted shank bone) — the Pesach (sacrifice) that protected the Israelites from the tenth plague

Chazeret (bitter vegetable, typically celery or romaine lettuce; Sudock knitted celery stalks)

Charoset (sweet paste made from dried fruit, nuts, and wine) — the mortar used by the Israelites in their labor for the Egyptians

Karpas (parsley) — a representation of the humility of servitude

Maror (horseradish root) — a symbol of the pain of servitude

Three matzohs

Why is this night different from any other? Sudock's knitted Seder plate. *Photo by Leslie Sudock, TikkunArts (Philadelphia, Penn.)*

But that ain't all. "In addition," says Sudock, risking brain explosion in her agog listener, "I made items which appear on Seder plates in many liberal and/or progressive Jewish households, including a potato (in memory of Holocaust privation and loss), a roasted beet (a vegetarian alternative to the roasted shankbone), and an orange (acknowledging gays and lesbians and others who are marginalized within the Jewish community). And my own personal additions to the Seder plate and table: an olive branch, in recognition of the shared suffering of the Palestinian people and their experience of loss of homeland; and a set of orange chains, in recognition of human rights violations worldwide." Uh, she's not done yet.

"I also knitted a version of the cup for Elijah and a few of the foods typically served by my Ashkenaz (European Jewish) family: matzoh ball soup, gefilte fish and hard-boiled egg, (flourless) chocolate torte/cake. Finally, I made a set of pieces representing the ten plagues, and a reversible chicken-and-egg, in recognition of the 'unborn egg soup' my grandmother and her sisters described to me when I was young." Nope, she *still* isn't done.

"In 2009, I added a set of the items used in the *bedikat chametz* (housecleaning) ritual conducted before the holiday begins: a candle, a wooden spoon, and a feather ... to 'sweep up' any remaining crumbs of prohibited leavened foodstuffs. And lastly, I sent a peaceful 'Paschal Lamb' to my nieces

Left: *Elijah's Cup.* Right: *Gefilte Fish Platter. Photos by Leslie Sudock, TikkunArts (Philadelphia, Penn.)*

for the holiday this year—a Lamb Chop hand puppet … my young niece-lets are understandably concerned about the animal rights implications of the shankbone on the Seder plate, so Lamb Chop can represent that contingent as well."

Whew!

To make these items, Sudock, a fifty-year-old attorney and mother of two, used mainly worsted yarns—Peace Fleece, Patons Classic Merino, KnitPicks Wool of the Andes, Cascade 220, Araucania semi-solid wool, and Red Heart, as well as other yarns from her collection, "some of which date to my university study abroad in Scotland, and even bits and pieces left over from high school projects," Sudock marvels.

They were stuffed, as necessary, with bits of plastic bags, cotton batting, or polyester filling. Some were reinforced with wire. And pretty much every design—with the exception of the egg and Lamb Chop patterns, were of Sudock's own devising. Together, they represent hours and weeks and months of work, as well as Sudock's 2007 decision to knit her way "through Jewish tradition and ritual as part of my personal commitment to study."

Unsurprisingly, Sudock has plans—big plans, and they include more knitting. She is hoping to finish a "Miriam's Cup (to pair with Elijah's Cup, in recognition of women's equality in contemporary liberal Jewish practice) and a set of pieces exploring the 'Four Sons' tradition; depending on time, I'll also execute a set of pieces to illustrate the *Had Gadya* song typically sung at the Seder table. Eventually, all the items will find their way onto the pages of a knitted *Hagaddah,*" which, knitting enthusiasts can only hope, will also be viewable on Sudock's jam-packed blog.

Ten Plagues. Photo by Leslie Sudock,
TikkunArts (Philadelphia, Penn.)

23

FOOD KNIT

KIYOKO YOSHIKAWA

A Feast You Can Sink Your Knitting Needles Into!

In 2002, a remarkable little book was published in Japan and slowly trickled its way into the consciousness of certain Western knitting enthusiasts who frequent Kinokuniya and other Japanese bookshops with outposts in American cities. The book was titled *Food Knit*, and the name of its author was a mystery, unless you happened to have a Japanese-speaking friend who could conduct a little research for you, since it isn't featured on the cover (or anywhere on the book's pages either, for that matter).

The author turns out to be a Kyoto-born Yuzen kimono designer named Kiyoko Yoshikawa. After twenty years at her career (she was, in fact, born to it—the daughter of a Yuzen fabric dealer, she studied graphic design at university), she

Yoshikawa turns her needles to the creation of luscious Japanese eatables. *Photo courtesy of Kiyoko Yoshikawa*

One of Yoshikawa's scrumptious bento boxes, featuring *donburi*, rolled sushi, shrimp, *shiso* leaf, and other goodies. Opposite: A whole "roasted" fish. *Photos courtesy of Kiyoko Yoshikawa*

longed for another outlet for her "handcrafting passion." In 1995, she was given an assignment to knit tempura for a magazine. And the rest, as they say, is history—and a lauded history at that. She went on to win a number of prestigious awards for her gastronomic creations, including one from the renowned women's magazine *Kateigaho*. So famous has her food knitting become in her mother country that she has been able to devote herself full time to it; her work appears frequently in exhibitions, on television, and in magazines.

What's remarkable about Yoshikawa's food knitting is not so much the subject—knitters have been knitting food for generations—but the incredible detail, thought, and skill that has gone into its creation. This is a new kind of food knitting, one that elevates food knitting to a breathtaking art form.

Even a quick flip through *Food Knit* is enough to hook you. The usual knit offerings of pastries and fruits and vegetables are all represented. But the materials Yoshikawa has chosen for their construction so perfectly complement them that most other food knitting pales by comparison: a slightly shimmery gold blend for Asian pears; fine, pale mohair for lettuce leaves; velvety eyelash to stand in as the meringue topping for a tart. Yoshikawa describes her use of materials thusly: "When I knit, the yarns begin to open and show their original way of representing many forms. A single strand of yarn already has its own demeanor, but it can be transformed into quite a different figure by being knitted."

Browsing yarn shops, Yoshikawa will remark, "This is good for a fig; that variegated yarn is exactly the color of salami with black pepper." When she cannot find the right color yarn commercially, she dyes it herself, drawing on her experience in traditional kimono coloring techniques. She asserts quite simply, "I can make any color I want."

Beneath the exquisite materials lie the decisions Yoshikawa has first made about what to knit. When's the last time you saw knitted bento boxes filled with shrimp atop a layer of rice and shredded egg; chestnuts as you'd find them fallen off the tree, spiky on the outside but opening to reveal the smooth nuts within; a roast pork dinner surrounded by tiny vegetables; a whole fish scattered with herbs and nuts? This is the only fiber food guaranteed to make your stomach gurgle. Through what Yoshikawa calls "the magic of process," she creates nonedible edibles that sometimes defy even her own imagination. What she thought might be an egg "can become pudding or ice cream. The effect is sometimes beyond calculation."

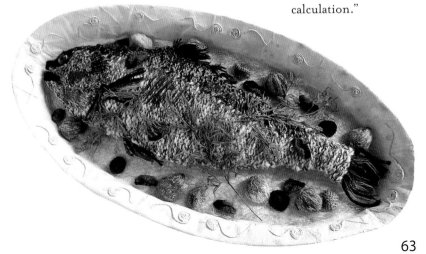

The Human Body

There are all sorts of things you can knit for your bod — and to represent it, inside and out.

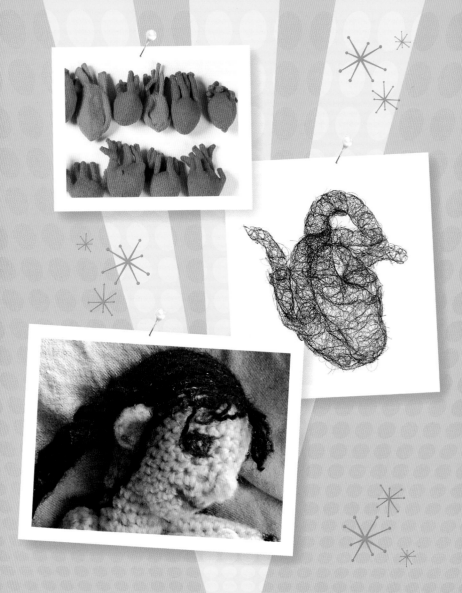

24

SUIT FOR A SKELETON

JIMINI HIGNETT

Knit Dem Bones!

If knitting a suit for a skeleton sounds like a ghoulish undertaking, consider the eclectic background of the "undertaker," England-born, Scotland-raised artist Jimini Hignett: children's party conjurer at the age of eleven; fire-eating-instructor at circus school at the age of fifteen; training to be a chimp for the movie *Greystoke* at seventeen; married in drag at age twenty. Knitting—knitting anything at all—seems tame by comparison.

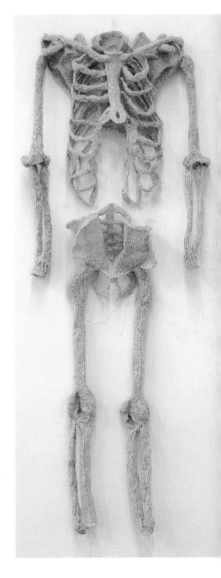

But when Hignett explains the whys and wherefores of *Suit for a Skeleton*, a life-size yarn creation that's been exhibited off and on since its inception in 2005, it seems downright commonsensical and touching—more in keeping with her current role as mother than with her experience in her early twenties as a court jester. The piece "can be read as a comment on the skeletal posture of today's fashion models; a wrapping of the inside as opposed to the outside; a simple comfort for the inherent coldness of the bones," she says. "It can touch on the way that mothers do not see their daughters. *'As long as you're dressed up nice and warm, dear'* Not noticing she's already become a skeleton."

continued on page 68

The *Skeleton*, all knitted up and ready to warm some bones. *Photo by Jimini Hignett*

I am a compulsive do-er and knitting was, and is, a way to make good use of otherwise wasted time. As well as knitting during school, I used to knit whilst waiting for the bus when I lived in London, or on the [subway] in New York. But now that I live in Amsterdam, I ride a bike everywhere, so those knitting moments have subsided, and anyway, the things I knit these days are mostly too complex to knit mindlessly whilst doing something else (the straight lengths of bones on the *Suit for a Skeleton* excepted). Other people in my family knit, too. My mother always has something on the go and used to invite friends round for an evening of knitting together—the idea of a sewing bee rekindled. When I lived in New York City, she brought me a magnificent pair of multicolored, striped, knobbly, baggy trousers, and the first day we went out with me wearing them, some millionaire uptown offered to buy them from me—we refused. My brother, too, knits, and of any of us, it is he who does the most traditionally complex things—Aran knitting with twisted rope patterns.

Previously, knitting and working with 'handicrafts' in general was part of a political statement (re)claiming 'crafts' as 'valid' art during which time various other textile-based skills such as quilting were appropriated by the feminist art movement. Then I suppose for a while any textile-based work had to deal with that legacy. Now I think that, in general, many artists do not feel limited to one particular medium or form, instead using the medium that is most appropriate for expression of the idea. For me, this is certainly the case—*Suit for*

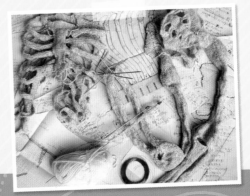

Hignett's *Suit for a Skeleton* in progress. Photo by Jimini Hignett

a Skeleton could not have been a painting or a ceramic. Or it could have been, but then it would be an entirely different work, which would be read entirely differently.

Traditionally, knitting was something done by men, too—that's certainly changed! Along with grandmothers knitting baby clothes, and hyper-expensive exclusive designer knits, I think there's a side to knitting that could perhaps be seen as subversive—after all, it's the antipathy of the *fast-fast-fast*, not-a-minute-to-spare society of today, and in that, a deliberate slowing down has a certain recalcitrance to it. This may be why it's sometimes viewed with a great sense of aggressive irritation, as if by simply knitting you are implicitly condemning someone else's high-speed lifestyle.

I'm not a purist as far as materials go; I tend to be practical. Because there's almost always a lot of trial and error [in my work], I tend to use cheap yarn—acrylic, whatever has about the right thickness and roughly the colors I envisage using. But if I need to be really subtle, then I have to buy from a proper wool shop where they have a wider range of matching colors.

My work often draws on contrasts and opposites. It is both funny and serious, attractive and repulsive, vulnerable and defiant. It is about what we see and what we do not see. What we feel and what we cannot allow ourselves to feel. Underlying everything are personal loves and attractions, aversions and indignities. It often deals with exposure: exposing complexity, complacency, complicity, and myself. Exposing *humanity in order to recover a place in it.*

My knitting has had a lot of positive reactions. People are moved by it, some even to tears. The topics are often not things you'd naturally discuss with strangers at an exhibition, so I like it

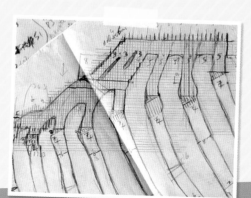

when the work draws people out and into discussion in this way. Obviously, I hope to change the world!

A detail of the *Skeleton* pattern. *Photo by Jimini Hignett*

continued from page 65

Suit for a Skeleton draws upon a deep well of emotion. And yet, as with all things made of knitting, there is a tremendous amount of practicality at the core of its construction. Using a double strand of acrylic yarn and copper wire in order to achieve enough stiffness in the suit to show that it was hollow, Hignett "wore great welts on my fingers." "I had to be careful not to get blood on the work." She improvised the pattern as she went, which proved tricky, as "the needles force the work to be flat along the knitted edge, even when the shape is intended to be round. It's hard to see it properly until you cast off, by which time, it's too late."

The first bit Hignett knitted was the pelvis, using as anatomy references her son Flint's how-to drawing book and a paper skeleton that hangs in their house. She worked her way up and down from there, attempting as much as possible to knit the suit in one piece. "The hardest part was the shoulder blades," she recalls. They had to be at once hollow, but also "give the impression of bone mass. There are pages and pages of trial and error with endless crossings-out and restarts and sketches for them. In the end I made a 3-D paper model and drew out the knitting grid on it in order to calculate where to increase and decrease."

Son Flint devised this crafty slogan for the potential buyer on the fence about the suit's functionality: "Does the wind blow through your ribs? Get this fantastic suit!" Well, winter's bound to come around sooner or later. What are you waiting for?

> The piece "can be read as a comment on the skeletal posture of today's fashion models; a wrapping of the inside as opposed to the outside …"

HELEN PYNOR

Lungs as Light as Air!

They are wispy and ethereal, the exact opposite of actual weighty, sloppy organs. Brain, heart, guts, lungs, all knitted up using single strands of human hair by Sydney-based artist Helen Pynor.

"When I [first] decided to knit with single strands of hair (surely an act of madness!), the images that came into my mind were garments, but these ideas gradually moved closer and closer to the internal body, going from coats, to hands, to lungs and a heart," says the knit-anatomist, who has a bachelor's degree in biology.

Before sitting down to knit in her studio, Pynor makes yarn by stranding together the hair of Spanish ladies sourced from a London dealer who supplies wig makers. The biggest challenge? Hair strands breaking. However, after stitching up all those organs, "I have a good feeling for the tension now."

"Being a trained sculptor (and self-taught knitter), I approach the process of constructing these pieces using the

continued on page 72

From Pynor, human organs knitted from human hair. *Untitled (heart lungs)*, 2007. *Courtesy private collection, Sydney, and Dominik Mersch Gallery, Sydney, photograph by Danny Kildare*

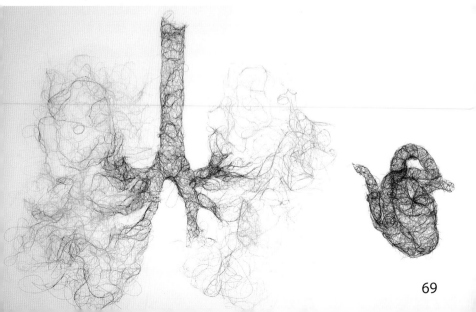

Profile

HELEN PYNOR

When I first worked with hair some years ago, I collected it in weekly rounds from all of the hairdressers within walking distance of my home at the time in Surry Hills, Sydney. This meant I ended up with a vast array of shades, textures, and lengths. Later, for the knitted works, I recognized that I needed long lengths of very high-quality hair. Living in Paris at [that] time, I sourced hair that met these exacting standards from a hair dealer in London, who supplies to wig makers and theater companies all over the world. The dealer was sourcing his hair from women in Spain, Eastern Europe, China, and India, who sell their hair to dealers. At times while I'm knitting these works, I wonder about the lives of the women who spent so many years growing these locks, and I think about how much personal history is tied up in the strands I am knitting.

There are no special processes I need to do to prepare the hair before I knit with it. However, I make sure that the hair is stored under the correct conditions, both before and after it is knitted (airtight and UV-proof containers made from an inert material). I use standard knitting needles, ranging from 3.5mm [size 4] through 9mm [size 13] and occasionally larger, depending on the finesse and detail of the piece I am knitting.

I use only stocking stitch for my knitted works, although with a knitting form that is so 'open air' and organic, it is difficult to identify the stitch type. I vary the needle size and the hair color to create different textures, densities, and translucencies. I create the hair 'yarn' by tying hair strands end to end to end. I usually make a long section of yarn first, followed by a spell of knitting. At different times I have had helpers to make the yarn—one friend in particular has made many yards of yarn for me, often sitting with me in my studio while I knit.

The forms are able to maintain their structural integrity with no additional treatment or sizing. Hair, whilst being a very delicate material, is also remarkably strong and resilient. Its natural spring, in combination with the hundreds of cross-over points that knitting creates, renders the forms quite strong and stable. I suspend the organs inside their display cases from either strands of blond hair or from very fine jewelry line, depending on the size of the piece.

It is clearly quite a challenging process to knit with such fine strands. I liken the process to a form of moving meditation—if my mind is still and calm, I can knit for hours with very little mishap. However, if my mind is agitated, I inevitably end up in a hair tangle at some point. It's a pretty accurate gauge of my state of mind at any given time! The other main challenge is seeing the hair visually. I solve this quite simply by using different colored papers on the desk underneath the knitting, which contrast with the color of the hair. Good light is also essential.

It is important that I respond to the sculpture and to the hair, rather than simply imposing my will. Hair has a habit of becoming very disobedient when I become willful with it, but it becomes magically cooperative when I work 'with' it. This can lead to unexpected surprises, when the hair reveals a form or a solution that prompts a different direction in the making process. Constructing these pieces demands a willingness to be observant of, and responsive to, what is unfolding and emerging.

Untitled (brain heart gut), 2007. Courtesy private collection, Melbourne, and Dominik Mersch Gallery, Sydney, photograph by Chris van der Spuy

continued from page 69

logic of sculpture," explains Pynor. She consulted visual aids such as photographs, anatomical diagrams in textbooks, and occasionally, real preserved organs. "I have learnt a lot about anatomy in the process!" Pynor laughs. While she aims to make the organs anatomically accurate, "at times, I also use metaphorical gestures that suggest aspects of the organs, rather than rendering them literally."

All the organs are knitted approximately to human scale, from a pattern. However, this is only a starting point. Says Pynor, "The process of knitting with single strands of hair is so organic that much of the making involves improvisation and responding to the way the form emerges as I knit and construct." As a final poetic act, a finished work is suspended from multiple strands of blonde hair.

A version of this entry first appeared in *Twist Collective* Fall 2010. Visit twistcollective.com

Left: *Exhale*, detail 2005. *Courtesy the artist and Dominik Mersch Gallery, Sydney, photograph by Danny Kildare*

Below: *Untitled (heart lungs, detail)*, 2007. *Courtesy private collection, Sydney, and Dominik Mersch Gallery, Sydney, photograph by Danny Kildare*

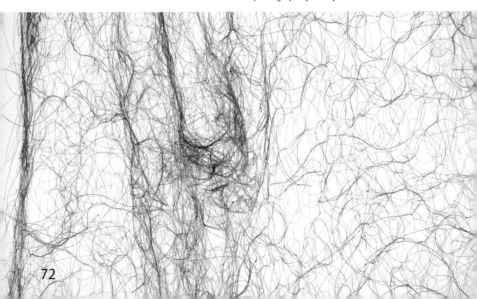

26
OBJECTS

IRIS EICHENBERG

More Hearts Than You Can Use in a Lifetime!

That's a whole lotta hearts—120 hearts in all—knitted up and stuffed by Dutch artist Iris Eichenberg using absolutely no pattern or initial sketch whatsoever. They may be anatomically correct—Eichenberg grew up on a farm, surrounded by animals and their parts; she's also trained as a nurse—but they are diminutive, each measuring only approximately 4 inches in diameter.

To achieve this scale, Eichenberg unravels standard skeins to get yarn as thin as possible, and knits the strands with five double-pointed needles of 1 millimeter thickness.

"Knitting," maintains Eichenberg, "is perfect to slowly grow an organic nonconstructed form. As the form evolves, I am able to control it millimeter by millimeter. To work forwards and backwards, allowing the work to literally grow out of my hands."

Each heart is meant to represent one of Eichenberg's friends or family members, and their illnesses and "malfunctions." And yet—how soft and lovely they are, and gorgeous, whatever their imperfections.

Whole lotta hearts: some of Eichenberg's knitted wool organs. *Photo by Travis Roozee*

73

CHILDBIRTH EDUCATION DOLL

SHARON COLEMAN

Really Gives Birth!
To Real Crocheted Newborn!

There was no sensationalism intended in the original birthing doll Rhode Island mom Sharon Coleman crocheted out of wool several years ago. "I designed it as an educational tool for my then-three-year-old daughter when I was pregnant with her little sister," she explains. But Internet responses to the pattern for the doll Coleman now sells on her Etsy shop ran the gamut—from simply surprised to downright disgusted.

The latter response strikes the average mom as slightly bizarre; after all, what could be more natural than childbirth? And for a crafty mom, what could be more natural than explaining the experience to her child using crochet?

 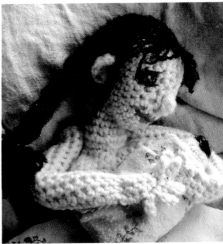

Left: Coleman's pregnant doll gives birth. Right: Together at last: mama and baby united. *Photos courtesy of Sharon Coleman, cozycoleman.etsy.com*

BREASTS FOR NURSING MOTHERS

DAWN THOMAS

Boobs Galore!

In September 2009 came the appeal: for boobs! And more boobs! A Lincoln, UK, midwife named Dawn Thomas was looking to assemble a stash. What the heck for? To teach other midwives how to train new moms the rudiments of nursing—to whit, when used in conjunction with a baby-size doll, how to achieve a good latch-on to "ensure that the baby has a good milk feed and that the mother does not get sore," according to Thomas, who is the Community Midwife Manager for the United Lincolnshire Hospitals NHS Trust. It's a prospect that's very welcome indeed to new nursing mothers confronted with hungry newborns.

The fake boob-as-training-tool is not a new idea, according to Thomas. Other wool-less and therefore less desirable models exist—those made of latex, for example, "have a very unusual, almost sticky feel to them," she says. "The knitted breasts are fun and a lot cheaper and easier to produce than those made of other materials."

Thomas has achieved her initial mission of providing knitted breasts to all the community midwives in her area and is working on distribution to other sites. The original boob stash was knitted by local residents, midwives, mothers, friends of midwives, and, says Thomas, "They have arrived in a variety of colors, shapes, and sizes. Striped, glittery, pink, and brown. We even have two that arrived with a note to say they were from a Martian. They are, of course, green."

Transformations

Who would you like to be today? Why not knit a whole new persona into being? Or at least, a whole new way to see the knitting universe that surrounds us.

29

SUPERHERO COSTUMES

MARK NEWPORT

World's Mightiest Knits!

Can a mere mortal artist ever be like a superhero? If the exploits of forty-seven-year-old Bloomfield Hills, Michigan, denizen Mark Newport are any indicator, the answer is yes: when he invents the valiant qualities he'd like to embody and then knits them into a costume. Thus are born the amazing Sweaterman! Bobble Man! Argyleman!

"In general," explains Newport, "I think of all these costumes as being made for me in the various roles I can take on, so I can protect my family. Sweaterman and the other [heroes] I have made up use the textures of knitting as the emblem of the suit. These pieces are questions about whether these things can be symbols of power. Can they embody the heroic?"

Good question. What *is* the protective quality of a bobble or a cable, anyway? Answers Newport: "Bobbleman is somewhat related to a kind of shaman's garment I used to see in galleries. It had fabric packets tied all over it, and those packets were said to contain the magic power of the shaman. So I thought of the bobbles

A knitted suit for Batman. *Batman 2: 2005. Courtesy of the Renwick Gallery of the Smithsonian American Art Museum.*

77

in that way, as well as a loss of power in the sense that it seems like his body is erupting with acne, so he is also *not* powerful. Cables suggest restraint and strength to me, and then they are generally used to form a pattern, which is unlike most superhero costumes. I also just plain enjoy the fact that moving a few stitches can change the look of the cloth in so many ways."

Long before there was Bobbleman and his all-powerful/powerless eruption of acne, however, there was Batman. This distinguished caped wonder occupied much of the first years of Newport's costuming—he's made four Batman suits to date. As he told Karen Searle for her book *Knitting Art*, what made Batman so fascinating was the fact that he was human, and "therefore vulnerable." And in fact, vulnerability seems written into the very fabric (no pun intended) of all Newport's fantastical togs. Says he: "My mom knit acrylic sweaters when I was a kid—not very many because she was a single mom with two boys and a job and going to school at night. So I use the same yarn she did—Red Heart worsted weight—and I feel that links my costumes to her protective gestures, which compare to the comic book hero actions which are the public side of protective gestures."

Such an explanation virtually nullifies any need to ask the question: why *knitted* (as opposed to sewn, or crocheted) costumes? Although Newport cites an entire laundry list of reasons. "Structurally," he says, "a knit cloth should stretch and move in a way that allows for active work, like that of a superhero. On the expressive side, [knitting] has contradictory associations to the idea of a superhero. Since knitting is generally associated with the feminine, and is quiet and meditative, it is the opposite of what we expect from comic book heroes, so that provides tension and a bit of humor to the work. I think the suits then ask people to think differently about knitting, heroes, men, and women, and to get past stereotypes or social norms. Another contradiction is that knitting is very time-consuming and quiet work," he continues, "where the hero is pictured acting impulsively and physically and dramatically."

Whatever qualities—protective, impulsive, or other—that Newport might epitomize when he morphs into Aquaman or the Rawhide Kid, they do not include the power to magically will his costumes into existence. Like other regular humans, he must knit them up, a process that takes between two and four months, although "since I switched from American to European knitting style, they are a little quicker to make." Their structure is "based on a raglan sweater pattern I found on the Internet," Newport says. "I used charts and formulas to make it fit me, then used measurements for the other elements. I added gloves to the arms, and an extended stocking cap for the hood. The legs get finished with socks."

As for challenges, "The part where the legs split is a bit tricky, because I usually like to use a pattern on it, and sometimes the counts need to be adjusted, and sometimes those textures make the fabric lie oddly."

Perhaps it's time to introduce the world to the talents of the Incredible Tailoring Man?

A knitted suit for the slightly … less-known *Argyleman* (2007), a superhero with decidedly diamondly powers. *Work appears courtesy of the artist; the Greg Kucera Gallery, Seattle, Wash.; and Lemberg Gallery, Ferndale, Mich.*

30

EVERYBODY IS SOMEBODY'S TERRORIST

ANDY DIAZ HOPE

Clowns Really Are Terrifying!

So are hippies, tourists, businessmen, and teenagers. It all depends on your perspective, and it's this simple consciousness shift that Andy Diaz Hope set out to explore post-9/11, when the word *terrorist* began to be thrown around "to marginalize dissenting voices and overpower dialogue." Says Diaz Hope, "When a representative of the government was calling a teachers' union a terrorist operation, I began to question the semantics of the word."

As envisaged by Diaz Hope, big business might be a terrorist in the minds of environmentalists; Greenpeace is

Have you seen these masked men? From left to right: Diaz Hope's *Clown Display, Hippy Display,* and *LA Tourist. Courtesy of the artist and Catharine Clark Gallery (San Francisco) and Schroeder Romero Gallery (New York)*

a terrorist in the minds of businessmen. "The aging baby boomers look at a group of teenagers and cross the street in fear; local economies in developing countries embrace busloads of fat tourists, while the local residents complain as their landscapes and livelihoods are replaced by private beaches and high-rise hotels they will never see the insides of. I tried to be as open as possible in my selection of groups," says Diaz Hope.

The terrorist balaclavas were knit up mostly of acrylic/wool yarns by a group of women in Bulgaria, who would riff on patterns sent by Diaz Hope, "adding details I wasn't sure were possible." Then each was worn to infiltrate an "enemy" group; the infiltrations were filmed, then edited into a video that was exhibited alongside the balaclava.

This initial group of terrorists is by no means encompassing. Says Diaz Hope, "I hope to add groups as time permits." Will knitters—potential airplane threats, with their barbs of wood and bamboo—be next?

31

LE CHAPELOU

ODE MARIE

Hideous! Adorable!

A visitor to a sixteenth-century Cabinet of Wonder—a highly personal sort of museum in which collectors assembled skeletons and rocks, paintings and books, jars and boxes of specimens of all varieties, some of dubious provenance—perhaps would not have been surprised to find within it the head of a monster such as Ode Marie created in 2008 with *Le Chapelou*. And in fact, such cabinets were Ode Marie's inspiration. "I liked the idea," she says, "of adventurers traveling in unknown countries and collecting unusual pieces."

This monster, though, which was inspired by certain African masks on display at the British Museum in London, has more in common with jewelry or other body ornament than with naturalist relics. Rather than frightening viewers, he is meant to be "reassuring,

Ode Marie's lonely monster, *Le Chapelou*, on the loose from his Cabinet of Wonder. From the collection *Cabinet of Curiosities*, 2008

friendly, amusing, and unexpected," says Ode Marie.

To accomplish his soft demeanor, the Normandy, France, native used mostly chunky yarns, mixed together for contrast; she crocheted his hair with green twine, knitted his teeth with tie-dyed yarn, and topped the whole head off with lace and plastic fruit to give "a final, precious touch."

This monster, like others of his ilk, may be more misunderstood than truly ogre-esque. Perhaps he's just lonely—one solitary monster, alone in his cabinet. But not for long—Ode Marie will soon stitch up a wife and children to join him.

32
CAT COAT

M'LOU BABER

Is It Inside Out? Or Right Side In?

And how did she make her knitting look like that, anyway?
The technique of double knitting (or colored double
knitting, in this case), was once a staple technique of
Scandinavian crafting. Fashioned by knitting with two strands
at once and twisting
the strands after each
stitch is formed, double
knitting creates a thick,
durable, and extremely
warm fabric—well,
two layers of fabric,
really, with a cushiony,
insulating air pocket
between.

"The stitches of
the two layers alternate
on the needles, and
for the simplest double
knitting, the stitches for
each layer are worked
with separate balls of
yarn," explains this
coat's designer, M'Lou
Baber. "But exciting
reversible color patterns
can be worked when
you interchange the
yarns for the two layers.
For double knitting
worked in stockinette

Baber's double-sided felines, seen from both
sides. *Double Knitting by M'Lou Baber from
Schoolhouse Press*

stitch, one 'stitch' represents two loops of yarn, or a pair.
One knit stitch will be of yarn A and a purl stitch of yarn B.
The knit stitch forms the right side of the fabric facing you,
the purl stitch forms the wrong side of the fabric facing away
from you. When instructions say to knit a particular number
of stitches, knit the knit stitch of the pair with one yarn and

purl the purl stitch with the other. In so doing, you work the rows of both layers at the same time."

Baber should know. She's been double knitting for almost twenty years, and judging by the remarkable garments in her 2007 book for Schoolhouse Press, *Double Knitting: Reversible Two-Color Designs*, she's pretty much mastered the technique—and then some.

"In October 1984, I picked up the holiday issue of *McCall's Needlework and Crafts* magazine and found a red and white afghan with Santa in his sleigh among the snowflakes. How could I resist?" wrote Baber in the book's introduction. She went from knitting this afghan to knitting more, and finally to designing her own patterns. Many of them, it turns out, involve cats. "Cats like me," says Baber matter-of-factly. "They show up in my yard. How can one not respond to that which jumps into our lap and purrs at us?"

The technique, no matter what pattern it's used to assemble, has its share of challenges. "Double knitting can be heavy and requires a loosely plied, lightweight yarn," says Baber. It also "produces a wide stitch, which makes swatching especially important." And how about this one? Baber is color blind. But the payoff, especially poignant to those who shun Fair Isle: no stranding!

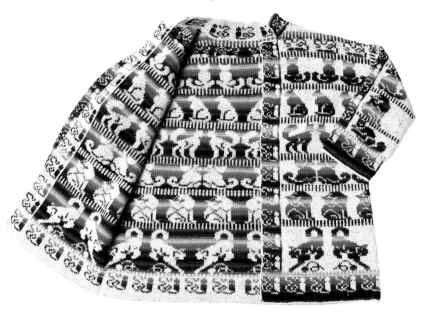

More double-sided cats to love. *Double Knitting by M'Lou Baber from Schoolhouse Press*

NARROW VISION

EVE JACOBS-CARNAHAN

Who Turned Out the Lights?

Looking at the world through rose-colored glasses is guaranteed to make it seem a sunny place. But what happens if you don a pair of *knitted* glasses? If they are the *Narrow Vision* glasses knit by Montpelier, Vermont–based artist Eve Jacobs-Carnahan, then likely you will not see much at all (beyond some tightly gauged homespun wool). And that's pretty much the point.

Says Jacobs-Carnahan, "*Narrow Vision* grows out of my reflections about how people choose to see what they want. I thought the juxtaposition of bright, wide eyes with narrowing blinders and eyes closed tight would be a fun way to encourage people to question their own perceptions."

Paradoxically, to knit something that's a commentary on lack of vision requires a certain clarity of vision. For Jacobs-Carnahan, this begins with sketches. "I'm

Seeing the world through knit-colored glasses: Jacobs-Carnahan's spectacles are guaranteed to give you "Narrow Vision." *Fiberart sculpture by Eve Jacobs-Carnahan; photo by Paul Rogers Photography, Stowe, Vt.*

a planner," she admits. "I start with a rough sketch of the general shape of the sculpture, with notes on the colors and textures." Next, she spins her own yarn, to her exacting specifications. "This allows me to choose the thickness, shine, and color," she says. Next, for *Narrow Vision*, she constructed an armature. "It was tricky to shape the wire structure without awkward intersections," she recalls. "The solution was to offset the intersections and join the blinders slightly inside the spot where the earpieces joined."

After that, "The knitting was easy!"

TEN UGLY HATS

DEBBIE NEW

Watch Them Spin!

Ugly? Maybe. But these hats have a thoroughly nontraditional function, thanks to the, well, machinations of Debbie New's brain.

Explains New, "This is one of a series of kinetic pieces that came about in response to my discontent with any effort to respond to sound or music in a static visual medium. I wanted to make some knittings that could be acted upon to cause movement and change." And so, of course, she did.

Knitted up of Philosopher's Wool donated to the project by Ann and Eugene Bourgeois, the "hats" and various structural accoutrements have been arranged into a kaleidoscope. Each of the ten hats is "individually ugly in that it is covered with random splotches of many colors," says New. "But in an array they display a symmetry and overall pattern for the eye to appreciate." They were knitted all at once on a large circular needle, five of a kind followed by five mirror images.

The best part of all? The kaleidoscope really works— turn the handle to set the rib/cogs in motion, then watch the thing spin. Ugly never looked so beautiful.

Pattern 1–6: Turn the crank to watch the pattern dance: New's *Ten Ugly Hats*." Photos by Debbie New

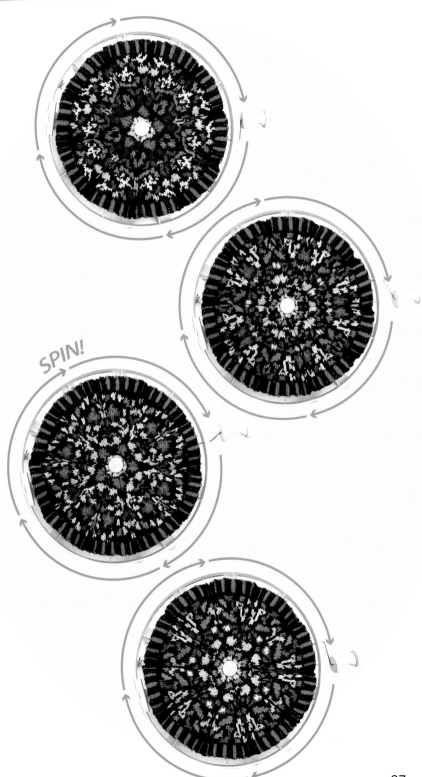

SPIN!

35

YARN BOMBING

KNITTAPLEASE

Cover Up That Parking Meter!

When it comes to the relatively new pursuit of yarn bombing (or knit bombing, or knitting graffiti, or guerilla knitting)—whether it be the wrapping of trees, or street signs, or gravestones—all influences point to KnittaPlease, the Austin, Texas—based tag team that's been wrapping around the world since 2005. The group was founded by Magda Sayeg, who claims the idea grew from a simple frustration with her unfinished knitting projects. And then it bolted from there. Lately, it has grown so far and wide that KnittaPlease's bombings have been spied on a Parisian sculpture, on parking meters in Brooklyn, New York, and on giant chess pieces in Sydney, Australia.

Keep your eyes peeled—they're probably coming to a city near you!

Knitting tags the whole wide world, including this bus in Mexico City, 2008.
Photo © Daniel Fergus

Above: Tricoteuses 07: playing a little footsy, in Paris, 2008. *Photo © Bergere de France*

Right: Covered chess pieces, Sydney, Australia, 2009. *Photo © Daniel Fergus*

Profile

KNITTAPLEASE

IN THE WORDS OF MAGDA SAYEG

Knitting is what I've always done.
I learned [to knit] in high school and
have continued to knit since. When
I began KnittaPlease, it came from my idea to beautify a door handle.
Knitting was my toolbox for this. That's how it started.

Part of the fun of KnittaPlease is that it takes this fuzzy, lovey
idea of knitting and applies it to the hard, masculine, aggressive
culture of street art. It confuses, because it doesn't fit into a neat
category. The objective is to beautify, to bring people back to an
awareness of their surroundings, of the fixtures that fill their worlds.

KnittaPlease used to work anonymously, but since the group
started receiving commissions [such as the '69 Meters' commission
in Brooklyn, New York, in the summer of 2009] and stopped working
exclusively at night, we've had the chance to see responses and
interact with the people who see our art. Some people are confused
by what I do. They don't understand the motivation or the purpose,
but they're so curious. Usually after this conversation, people just
chuckle, or thank me for adding some quirky beauty to their world.

I love how this movement resonates with so many people. Yarn
bombing claims relevance across cultural and national boundaries
because it addresses a commonality in every urban dweller's life around
the world. It calls attention to the need for beauty in our streets filled
with unexceptional gray cement and steel. Seeing a global community
form around this movement has confirmed my original vision, and I
have expanded my purpose to involve communities and other knitters
in my own projects. KnittaPlease has become, in many ways, about
drawing people together—across generations, nationalities, and
borders. There is so much potential here.

I'm always working on ideas to stretch KnittaPlease into new
territory. I wrapped a bus in Mexico City in November 2009, and I would
love to continue wrapping large scale. Maybe an airplane one day?

36
REKNIT

HAIK AVANIAN, GAYANE AVANIAN,
AND SVETLANA AVANIAN

When Is a Sweater *Not* a Sweater?

It's one of the oldest ideas in knitting: unraveling an old knit to make a new knit. Only graphic designer Haik Avanian and his mom, computer programmer Gayane Avanian, have kicked the whole concept up a notch. They've collaborated to create Reknit, a small, fledgling Internet "business" (quote marks there, because at $30 a pop, it's certainly less about making money than encouraging "my mom to partake in her hobby more often," Haik told the GOOD blog in March of 2010). It's purpose? Well … to *reknit*, of course: sweaters most commonly, but any old knitted item will do.

It works like this: You (and twenty-nine other first-come-first-served customers) send the Reknit team your worn-out or untrendy cardigan. You vote on what you'd like said cardigan to be turned into (one January it was scarves; February, fingerless gloves; March, hats). Haik's grandmother, Svetlana, devises a prototype. Gayane unravels and steams the yarn from each of the thirty old garments, then stitches them up according to Svetlana's template. Voilà! Your garment has been Reknit!

With Reknit, a sweater is unraveled….
Idea Credit: Gayane Avanian, Design: Haik Avanian, Photography: Ani Avanian

The repurposing of yarn has a long and venerable history in the Avanian family. The jackets Svetlana knit for Gayane and her sister when they were born were eventually unraveled to make one sweater for Gayane, then unraveled by Gayane years later to knit herself a dress, again to knit Haik's baby sister a sweater and pants set, and yet again to knit a jacket for the same sister several years later. Recently, though, "We had sort of exceeded the threshold of knit"—and reknit—"items in our family and there was no longer a need for this outlet." The only hope for Gayane and her knitting passion was to outsource it. And how especially fortunate for each month's lucky thirty that she has.

… And the yarn gains a second life as a scarf.

37

DOUBLE KNIT STOCKINGS

BEVERLY ROYCE

A Sock *Inside* a Sock!

There's been a lot of knitting world hullabaloo over the years about the origins of socks constructed with double knitting— that is to say, in this instance, two socks knit at the same time, on the same set of needles, one inside the other. Beverly Royce, who devised a pattern for them in her book *Notes on Double Knitting* for Schoolhouse Press, named them "Anna Makarovna's Secret Stockings." This title was an homage to the first-known reference to the stockings, in Leo Tolstoy's *War and Peace*, which was first published in Russia in 1869.

To a roomful of cheering children, Anna Makarovna reveals her completed stockings, described by Tolstoy thus: "This meant two stockings, which by a secret process known only to herself Anna Makarovna used to knit at the same time on the same needles, and which, when they were ready,

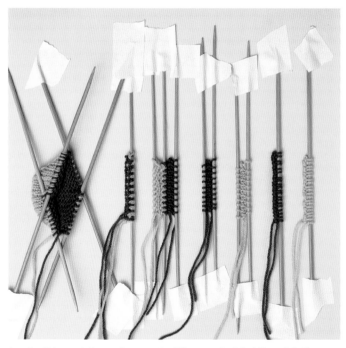

A sock within a sock: impressive every time! Photographs © *Jack Deutsch for Vogue Knitting International Magazine (Spring/Summer 1987)*

she always triumphantly drew, one out of the other, in the children's presence."

Several years later, in 1875, such double-knit stockings appear in a U.S. patent, granted to Frederich Polle, Louisa Keisker, and Sallie Polle. The trio give instructions for everything—except, critically, how to shape the heels and toes, and how to reduce and increase, which online knitting-patent-watcher The Girl from Auntie calls "the trickiest part of the double-knit sock trick." But they do offer one thing no one else does: directions for knitting not only two socks at once, but four socks at once. *Alors!*

These days, if you have a hankering to make a sock in a sock, you can follow Beverly Royce's pattern. But bear in mind this caveat, from Royce herself: "Please do not presume that I'm presenting this method as an excellent way to knit a pair of socks. It is a good way to test skills, mystify friends, challenge knitting abilities and patience, and amuse children." Scant praise indeed, for a technique that dazzles nevertheless.

95

KNITJAPAN

YOSHIMI KIHARA

Turning Real Live Housewives into Knitting Artists!

"What would happen if you took a small group of ordinary Japanese women and housewives with a common enthusiasm for knitting, and tried to get them to look at their hobby from the point of view of professionals or artists?" This was the unusual premise of a series of workshops led by London-based Japanese knitwear designer Yoshimi Kihara. Surely, many crafting housewives have dreams and aspirations beyond the confines of their home-based workrooms. Many aspire, but few manage anything like celebrity.

Not so for the eighteen women Kihara drew to her annual workshops beginning in 1990. They studied, they knit, "each trying to push and tug at the limits of their individual skills and abilities," wrote Kihara. In 2001, Kihara organized their collective work into an exhibition, under the title *Fushiginoiroito*—meaning "puzzling, strange, mysterious," and "colored yarns." The exhibit treated visitors to London's Knitting and Stitching Show to a large dollop of exquisite contemporary Japanese knitting. There, reports Kihara, they stood beside their work to meet the public and "were astonished by the enthusiasm and respect with which they were met."

So, they did it again. Back they traveled to the Knitting and Stitching Show in 2005. Only this time, their work was exhibited alongside that of established Japanese textile artists and designers, in order that "the safety net of being enthusiastic amateurs has been removed," read the show's accompanying brochure. No pressure, ladies!

Admittedly, the women of *Fushiginoiroito* are still not household names here in the States. But take a gander at their website: www.knitjapan.co.uk. Decide for yourself if the dazzling red wool/silk/cotton/rayon garments of Mieko Asada, and the highly textural pantaloons of Mari Nakayama, and the rippled, multicolored coat of Toshiko Hayashi don't deserve a bit of knitting-world renown.

Creature Knitting

First there was knitting for humans. Then for their dogs. And finally, their … penguins? Not to mention knitting the actual penguins themselves.

39

SWEATERS FOR ... PENGUINS?

PHILIP ISLAND NATURE PARK

Swaddle Your Water Birds in Knitwear!

Yes, penguins! And those waddly water birds certainly elicit "oohs" and "awws" by the dozens when they're outfitted in their bright, knitted "jumpers" (as they're known Down Under). But extreme cuteness, though an obvious side effect, is far from the point of the exercise. In fact, the sweaters are a device integral to saving the lives of Australian Little Penguins that have been coated in oil from tanker spills. The sweaters are a simple solution to a deadly problem. Penguins caught in such a spill will preen their feathers in order to clean them, thereby ingesting the toxic oil. The sweaters merely eliminate the penguins' access to their own feathers until they are strong enough to receive a washing with warm water and detergent. In the last two cases of Little Penguin rescue orchestrated at Philip Island in 2001 and 2003, the organization achieved an enormous success rate in rehabilitating the oiled birds, thanks in no small part to the sweaters. Of 463 birds oiled in those years, 98 percent were released back into the wild.

Penguin sporting a knitted jumper—clean, dry, and warm. *Photos courtesy of Penguin Foundation: Philip Island Nature Park*

The sweaters were first conceived of by Marg Healy, a rehabilitation officer at the Philip Island Nature Park, a not-for-profit wildlife conservation site founded by the State Government of Victoria. The urgent need for them arose in 1998, when 1,000 liters of bunker oil from a never-identified tanker was discharged into the Bass Strait close to shore. Healy had seen sweaters used on oiled English guillemots (another type of seabird), and with the help of a local knitter, she came up with several adaptations for penguins.

Says Healy, "We went through about six prototypes before we got a really good one. We developed it further through the years, to the point where we now have elastic added to the bottom hem and neckline, because the penguins worked out that if they put their toenails through the hem and walked forward, the jumper would slide down their bodies" and they could step right out of them.

Knit your own Penguin Jumper with the pattern on page 229!

If you're thinking of stitching up a sweater in the hopes that it will clothe a penguin in need, don't bother. Over the years, Philip Island has received so many Little Penguin sweaters they now report a surplus. (Most notable among the offerings: several full sets of Australian Football League sweaters and a complete wedding party ensemble, consisting of a layered lace dress and tuxedo.) The extra sweaters are now sold in their gift shop in order to raise money for the island's wildlife hospital.

Cleaning an oiled penguin at Philip Island Nature Park.

PENGUIN

KIYOKO YOSHIKAWA

Even More Adorable Than the Real Thing!

As if knitting up exquisite foodstuffs (see page 61) weren't enough of an accomplishment, the *Food Knit* lady is back—with penguins. Yeah, penguins. And we challenge you to find them any less lifelike, or appealing, than the Philips Island rescue-ees featured earlier.

"I feel lucky about it," Yoshikawa says about the endeavor for which she was contracted by Japanese sportswear company Descente (one of whose brand trademarks is, of course, a penguin). The company used the woolen bird in various publicity materials. Says Yoshikawa of her knitting career, "I've got the opportunity to go on to a new stage."

But the real question is: Does a knitted penguin ever require a knitted penguin jumper?

Yoshikawa's knitted penguin is a dead ringer for the real thing. *Photo courtesy of Descente and KiyokoYoshikawa*

BEYOND DARWIN: BIODIVERSITY RECLAMATION SUITS FOR URBAN PIGEONS

LAUREL ROTH

Avian Must-Haves for an Eco-Conscious Era!

Ever wish there were fewer pigeons and more, say, condors in your neighborhood? San Francisco–based artist Laurel Roth has got the solution: crocheted "suits" to disguise our nation's winged urban pests as more savory, albeit extinct, members of the avian community. In this way, we can re-create a seriously faltering biodiversity and "soothe our environmental fears," says Roth, all in one neat little package.

So, instead of looking out with ennui and irritation at a streetful of crumb-scavenging pigeons, we may instead feast our eyes upon a panoply of dodos, ivory-billed woodpeckers, passenger pigeons (a wholly different, once-wild, and considerably more useful type of pigeon altogether), and, yes, those condors mentioned previously—all of which have long died out.

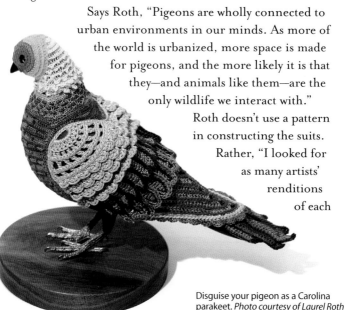

Says Roth, "Pigeons are wholly connected to urban environments in our minds. As more of the world is urbanized, more space is made for pigeons, and the more likely it is that they—and animals like them—are the only wildlife we interact with."

Roth doesn't use a pattern in constructing the suits. Rather, "I looked for as many artists' renditions of each

Disguise your pigeon as a Carolina parakeet. *Photo courtesy of Laurel Roth*

bird as possible (no photos of live birds in most cases). I did a few sketches to try and get a basic plan of stitches and patterns and colors. Then it was freehand trial and error. They've gotten more complex as I've learned. After the first one—the dodo—I learned to make the mannequin first, so that I can test the fit as I go."

Materials are a highly specific hodgepodge of fine yarn and crochet and embroidery threads. "I probably have a bit of an odd reputation at my local yarn shop for coming in every few months and lurking around touching every yarn until I pick what must seem a totally mismatched set of yarn," confesses Roth. "They'll ask if they can help me, but I feel a little awkward about asking if they have anything in the green of a Carolina parakeet's neck with a super-fine gauge and a slight iridescent sheen, or something reminiscent of the ruff of a condor's neck."

The pigeons, though, may be glad for her efforts. "I like the idea that maybe the pigeons are using the suits as part of their adaptation to make us appreciate them. As extinct animals, they get to feel special, maybe have stamps made in their likeness," she says.

Or why not disguise your pigeon as a dodo (left), or a passenger pigeon (above)? *Photos courtesy of Laurel Roth*

42

ANIMALS

PATRICIA WALLER

Man-Eating Crochet!

Today, she can crochet an entire taxidermy deer head. But Patricia Waller's first fiber work—a knitted oven mitt she made in grammar school in Germany at the age of nine— "looked so awful that my mom put it in the garbage," she confesses. "I think you can see, my technique has improved."

Improved, yes—and greatly expanded over the years to include myriad members of the animal community: crocodiles, elephants, unicorns, and sharks. Only these don't compose a cute, cuddly menagerie. More often than not, they're victims of grisly accidents—albeit, crocheted accidents—or responsible for them. The shark's got a bloody leg between its teeth; the crocodile, an entire child; the unicorn has impaled a teddy bear with its horn; the elephant's howdah is fastened directly into its back. They are meant to "play with various themes we usually prefer to ignore," explains Waller. "Fears of aging, illness, and frailty, barely concealed cravings for sensation, irrational phobias, dangerous desires. Cute stuffed animals are revealed, on closer inspection, to be freaks."

Each one takes several months to create—with no pattern, but plenty of consideration given to material (usually acrylic, which doesn't fade in the sun and is mothproof). Bearing in mind, as Waller quips, "Not every red yarn is good for blood." The time and effort are worth it, though; Waller is pleased to be crocheting up a paradox—making things by hand in a time of mass production. "Knitting and crocheting both allow for creating something individual to provoke our imagination and fantasy," She says. Monkey rowing a giant banana, anyone?

Waller's cuddly crocheted menagerie might just as soon eat you as look at you (*Crocodile*, page 103). In Waller's mysterious land, an elf (top) has the head and torso of a woman and, cruelly, the hindquarters of a snail. This monkey (above) is happy to paddle himself (*Rowing Monkey*). © Patricia Waller

43

KNITTING WITH BEAR HAIR

MAXINE TYLER

Possibly the Most Dangerous Knits in the World!

Up in New Hampshire, they're knitting with hair from black bears. Well, at least one woman is: eighty-one-year-old Maxine Tyler, the Official Bear Knitter of Clark's Trading Post. Three bears at the Post—whose family of owners has been putting on bear shows since 1949—have been combed for yarny purposes, yielding what *Piecework* magazine calls a "somewhat scratchy" fiber that gets spun into singles (for kids' knits) or two-ply.

Alas, the end products—mostly mittens and hats—are not for sale. You must be a friend of the bears to rate.

Willa Clark wears her sweater, knit by Maxine Tyler using hair from a bear named Ursula. *Photo by Maureen S. Clark, Clark's Trading Post*

KNITTING WITH PET HAIR

KENDAL CROLIUS

Not for the Allergy Ridden!

You may not have a bear to comb for fiber, but there's a good chance you have a shedding dog or a cat … or better yet, a soft, cuddly angora rabbit! The idea of knitting with its fur surfaces every now and again—to whit, Kendal Crolius' 1994 book on the subject, and a recent Asheville, North Carolina, company called Pet Yarn Chic, which contracted spinners and knitters to create pet-hair fashions from Fido and Fluffy.

And why not? In one fell swoop, you could rid yourself of hair bunnies and stitch up a garment to keep you warm. The only problem, as the *Los Angeles Times* reported on Pet Yarn Chic's offerings: These knits shed.

Spinning luxuriously soft angora yarn right off the rabbit's back. *Photo © Wendy Johnson*

DARWIN'S LEFTOVERS

LIZ LANCASHIRE

Caressable Creepy Crawlies!

On first consideration, there was nothing truly exceptional about the exhibit on view at the Bristol Zoo Gardens in England in summer 2009. Tarantulas, beetles, hummingbirds, iguanas, fossils, and tortoises: pretty standard fodder for a commemoration of the 200th anniversary of Charles Darwin's birth. But this selection of natural phenomena was possessed of a certain feature that the eminent biologist could never have foreseen. It was, from its smallest antenna to its largest exoskeleton, fashioned entirely out of knitting.

Led by artist Liz Lancashire, a team of sixty knitters from across Gloucestershire hunkered together to stitch up the woolly menagerie. Said Lancashire, "Charles Darwin had many hundreds of stuffed animals in his cupboard, and I wanted to re-create some of the paraphernalia of his scientific collection and capture the day he had a clear-out!" Yarn was donated to the group by Patons, and the project was funded by the National Lottery.

Lancashire hopes these efforts will help save one *human* subgroup from extinction. "My aim is to spread understanding about Darwin's key ideas and to reawaken people's interest in knitting," she says. "Fifty years ago most women would have been confident knitters making [most] of their own clothes. Now knitting is on a par with other hand-based skills such as dry-stone walling, and expertise is being lost with each generation."

A dearth of expertise, however, was certainly not in evidence amid the marvelous menagerie in Bristol.

The One and Only Jan Messent

Since the 1980s, knitters have been discovering and rediscovering the whimsical, delightful creations of Jan Messent.

HAVE YOU ANY WOOL?

In yarn stores everywhere, knitters can be spied pulling one of Messent's eight knitting books from a shelf and suddenly proclaiming, "Look at this! It's Queen Elizabeth! Here's a whole castle, with knights! I can knit a basket of vegetables!" How do you tally the value of her work? It isn't easy to decide—because of her, Brit Fiona McDonald's aliens and Irene York's cacti (see page 141) are possible. So we've given her five entries: one for each of her five best-known knitting books.

During the 1980s and 1990s, sponsored by what she terms "the big yarn-spinners of the UK" who were concerned that teachers were not teaching knitting, Messent was paid to do just that. "This brought in some funds of which I was in very short supply at the time," she recalls. And because she also made line drawings and diagrams for books published by Search Press, this led to a book of her own, her first about knitting, titled *Have You Any Wool?*, published in 1986.

In the book, she encouraged knitters to use their leftover oddments of yarn to knit up sheep and shepherds, dice and dominoes. As a result, she opened up a previously unexplored avenue to creative and simply orchestrated needlework projects.

From *Have You Any Wool?* A cobra ready to strike. *Knitting by Jan Messent, photo courtesy of Search Press*

Messent, currently in her seventies and living in a town on England's southern coast, was hired next by Search Press to rewrite, re-knit, re-pattern, and redraw Dane Hannelore Wernhard's classic little book, *The Knitted Farmyard*. "It is from this wonderful little book that the other whimsy ideas grew: gardens, fantasy, figures," she says. To whit: *Wool 'n' Magic*, the next book she authored in 1989, an odd and distinctly personal offering that aimed to encourage needleworkers to "try unconventional projects," according to *Publisher's Weekly*. If you were keen to stitch up highly textural wall hangings, soft sculptures of mermaids, or caves replete with stalagmites and stalactites, this was the book for you.

> "It is from this wonderful little book that the other whimsy ideas grew ..."

A stalactite cave adds beauty and mystery to the pages of *Wool 'n' Magic*. Knitting by Jan Messent, photo courtesy of Search Press

48
KNIT A FANTASY STORY

Messent's whimsy took on a distinctly childlike air with *Knit a Fantasy Story*, also published in 1989. This book was actually a re-release of three books in one: Wernhard's *The Knitted Farmyard* as well as two of Messent's own authorship that had gone out of print. Its three sections were aimed not only at adults seeking to knit something fantastical for their kids but at older kids who might be inspired to knit a little something for themselves. The farmyard section was a prelude to Messent's own *Knitted Gardens* (see next page); the section that was once a book titled *Knit an Enchanted Castle* boasts not only the red-roofed castle itself but the jousting knights, ladies, and dragons to inhabit it; and the section that was *Knitted Gnomes and Fairies* offers up a menagerie of mythical creatures, such as unicorns and, naturally, gnomes and fairies. As a whole, it managed to accomplish what Messent most hoped: knitters drawn to this book did not merely copy her designs verbatim but used them as jumping-off points for their own imaginations.

A knitted enchanted castle from *Knit a Fantasy Story* is almost as good as the real thing. *Knitting by Jan Messent, photo courtesy of Search Press*

KNITTED GARDENS

This charming little book, released in 1991, is usually the first of Messent's that American knitters stumble upon at their local yarn store, and its appeal is undeniable. Messent stretched its theme in a variety of directions. There are tiny vegetables (carrots, rutabagas, cabbages) and farm animals (sheep, rabbits, chickens) that can be knitted individually to delight tiny recipients. There are blankets and pillow covers that can be covered with garden scenes or even rows of produce and flowers to mimic an actual backyard scenario.

Best of all, there are miniature tabletop gardens: cottage gardens with neat rows of hedges and shrubs, water lily ponds, fountains, and planting beds; friary gardens with bee skeps, cold frames, archways, and doves; and "modern" gardens with planting pots, topiaries, watering cans, benches, and compost sacks. Naturally, there are small knitted people to tend to the bounty: farmers and ladies and children and friars.

There's something for every sort of gardener in *Knitted Gardens*: tidy plots between cottages, bee skeps, and cold frames of lettuces for friars. *Knitting by Jan Messent, photo courtesy of Search Press*

KNITTED HISTORICAL FIGURES

The bland title of this wonderful book, Messent's last on knitting, published in 1992, does not do it justice. Showing knitters how to create a body template from yarn-wrapped wire covered with a knitted "skin," Messent proceeded to embellish that body in twenty-one amazing ways, spanning the centuries. She conjured Egyptian men and women, with snake headdresses and golden sandals; an Italian Renaissance lady wearing an open-work gown, lacy petticoat, and gartered socks; King Henry VIII and Queen Elizabeth I in all their courtly finery; simply clad pilgrims; and a ruffly Madame de Pompadour.

The irony of all this creative knittery? Messent doesn't consider herself much of a knitter at all. She's an embroiderer first and foremost, and she began publishing books on that topic in 1976. "I preferred to use embroidery as a more exact representation of the real me," says Messent, a little sheepishly. ("This sounds pretentious—we Brits *hate* pretentiousness.") Well then, it's lucky for us that she discovered her knitting muse.

Why knit a person when you could knit a historical person? Here's Queen Elizabeth I, from *Knitted Historical Figures. Knitting* by *Jan Messent, photo courtesy of Search Press*

Seaworthy

Once upon a time, sailors wore knitted guernseys to protect them from the elements. Knits-of-the-sea sure have come a long way, ye hearties!

51

COAT FOR A BOAT

INGRID WAGNER

Knitting That Floats!

Why knit a coat for a boat? Why not? Especially if you are looking to involve as many segments of your river-bound community as possible in a giant, encompassing art project that combines two seemingly disparate and unrelated crafts.

The project was the brainchild of Esen Kaya, an English visual arts developer who tapped the talents of artist and self-proclaimed "Big Knitter" Ingrid Wagner, as well as 350 other knitters in her nautical plot. First, a 21-foot historical coble boat was custom-made by the North East Maritime Trust, which is "committed to preserving the skills associated with building wooden boats which once fished the River Tyne," explains Wagner. Then it was covered bow to stern in knitting and displayed at Kaya's gallery for a month before being launched into the River Tyne in July 2009 as part of the Mouth of the Tyne Festival. Each knitted plank was treated with

Building the boat: First thing's first—boat builders with the North East Maritime Trust construct a 21-foot historical coble boat. *Photo used courtesy of the artist*

water repellent, then glued and stapled to the boat, which itself was cut into four sections so that it could be taken in and out of the gallery.

The undertaking was simply enormous, and to achieve it, volunteer knitters were encouraged to use a combination of traditional needles and Wagner's Big Knit Needles, for speedier results. Of the core group, who met to knit every Saturday for four months, twelve knit the actual cover for

the boat, using needles nearly 16 inches (400mm) long and recycled and dyed bed sheets donated by a nearby hospital. Other Saturday knitters used large or small needles and patterns devised from the project's "resident expert," Doctor Sue, who could "simply take one look at a painting featuring medieval dress and reproduce it in knitted form. Shrimps, lobsters, and seals were just some of the creatures created in pattern by Doctor Sue." The 13-foot sail for the boat was knit in an astonishing five days by textile students who found the project "exciting because it was so different," Wagner reports.

Accompanying the boat covering and its sail was an astonishing range of all-knitted nautical items, some using materials unusual to your average knitter but essential in Wagner's world of Big Knitting: raffia, telephone wire, plastic bags, garden twine, foil, paper, velvet, and voile. Although the project was originally intended to be local in scope, news of it spun round the globe. A team in Australia sent jellyfish; France sent a telescope; New York sent porpoises. A blind knitter made a fishing net, and a community of partially sighted knitters made a sand carpet and cliff face.

Each knitted plank was treated with water repellent, then glued and stapled to the boat ... The undertaking was simply enormous ...

There was an enormous seascape knit from cut fabric. There was a fisherman's washbag, complete with soap, washcloth, and books of "chat-up lines." There was a plate of fish and chips, a ship's cat with mouse in tow, crabs, an entire shoal of fish, a stopwatch, lobster pots, seagulls, boots, a ship's anchor, knitted rope, rocks, pebbles, and oars. It was, admits Wagner, a "slightly mad" project. But "sometimes the route to discovering what one is capable of ... requires a willingness to take a risk and create."

Wagner with the completed boat and a panoply of (knitted) objects and animals from the briny deep. *Photo used courtesy of the artist*

52

KNITTED PLANKTON

ANITA BRUCE

Is That Knitting Caught in My Hair?

Summer beach swimmers would certainly be pleased to surface from beneath the waves with one of Anita Bruce's knitted creations wrapped tendril-like around them. The artist, who has a first degree in zoology, knits "hypothetical" plankton and other sea forms that resemble anemones, starfish, and jellyfish, some of which are straight out of nineteenth-century scientific drawings.

> "I'm really trying to champion biodiversity and highlight the range of exotic and fanciful creatures ..."

Before stitching them up from 0.25mm enameled copper wire, Bruce designs her plankton on paper, sketching out a diagram of the form she wants to make, often with notes about how she

Bruce's Knitted Plankton from her Mutation Series riff on real-life sea forms.
Photography by Anita Bruce

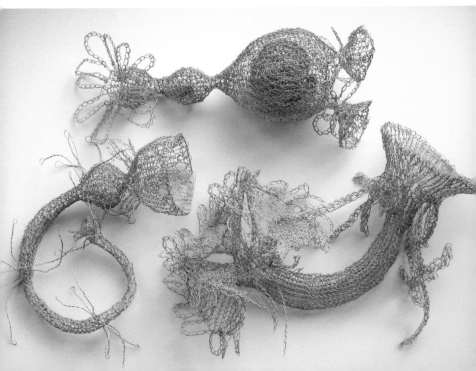

Silver Darlings swim through the air, barely rippling their shadows. *Photography by Anita Bruce*

will join sections together. "I often work spherical forms inside one another, so I have to think carefully about the sequence as I work them in to avoid flattening the inner shapes," she explains. "The knitting comes off the needle flat, so I have to make sure I design in openings so that I can form the shapes, and have a range of tools for this job." The most useful: her bulb dipper!

Bruce's wirey amorphous forms aren't meant merely as luxurious ornaments. "I'm really trying to champion biodiversity and highlight the range of exotic and fanciful creatures that inhabit the earth and the need for us to protect their environments," she asserts. "If we think of the amazing, unimaginable creatures that are being discovered from very deep seas that we didn't know existed until recently—these are the life forms I'm celebrating."

53

CORAL

INGA HAMILTON

Nothing Endangered about These Crocheted Reefs!

British crafter Inga Hamilton has a passion: a passion for coral, that is. Especially if she can crochet it *big*! (See her world-record crochet hook claim on page 224.)

"I was awaiting surgery, amassing a section of things to help me through the boredom of a three-month recovery period," she recalls. "I bought a set of steel sculpting tools at auction, and at the bottom of the box was a very old steel crochet hook. I grabbed a ball of deep purple chenille and crocheted a huge anemone top to a padded coral sculpture that I'd been working on, that had been missing the final touch." And that, dear reader, is how crocheted coral mania is born.

Since that time, Hamilton's gone on to crochet not just the tops but entire coral reefs. During her recovery period alone, she created five 16-foot coral reefs in various color

Hamilton's crocheted wonder: *Great White Reef*. Photo © rockpool candy/Inga Hamilton

schemes. Then she set about creating smalle[...] up her recovery clinic.

She makes it all up as she goes along. "It's a[...] running after you've had a few drinks," she quips[...] roughly where you want to go, but you're not sure [...] steps it'll take or quite which direction your legs wil[...] you." Not to mention, "I would never be so bold as t[...] replicate Mother Nature. She's the expert."

Hamilton's crocheted wonder: *Pink Reef.* Photo © *rockpool candy/Inga Hamilton*

ABOVE AND BELOW THE WAVES

ALISON MURRAY

Now You Can Walk Over and Under the Water!

First, she oversaw the knitting of a 60-foot Christmas tree. Then, an entire life-size gingerbread house, replete with garden and furnishings (see page 30). Now British knitter Alison Murray has shed her holiday fixation and is back with her most ambitious project to date: *Above and Below the Waves*, a phantasmagoria of starfish and jellyfish, seaweed, mermaids, crabs, shells, boats, a beach, and a lighthouse. And once again, knitters from all over the globe have been inspired to pony up their needles and send in their creations. In 2010 and 2011, the project toured the UK in an effort to raise money for the Royal National Lifeboat Institution—at least, enough of it to train one lifeboat crewman for a year.

Up from the fishy deep: a mermaid and a series of rays. *Photos courtesy of Alison Murray*

SEA URCHINS

PATRICIA BOWN

Just Like Real Life, with No Fishy Odor!

Here are sea urchins (sixty-four sea urchins, to be precise), yarny replicas of the watery *echinoidea* class, stitched up by Brit Patricia Bown in 2008 for a "Jonah and the Whale"—themed arts festival. "I was only going to make a few, but once I started, I couldn't stop," admits Bown sheepishly.

"Each one became unique because I experimented with scale, form, and combinations of yarns, finishing with a variety of hand embellishments."

Indeed, yarn combinations were integral to Bown's goal of absolute realism. "Yarns which are space-dyed can result in a regular color pattern when knitted up, which I didn't want," says Bown, a

Sea urchins galore, more than you could fit in a knitted bucket. *Photo courtesy of Patricia Bown*

former occupational therapist who received her B.A. in textiles from Manchester Metropolitan University in 2007. "There are lovely yarns available, but in some cases I had to use two or three yarns together to emulate the true color or texture [of the sea urchin.] As the combination is knitted up, the yarns twist round, which gives a random, but realistic color variegation."

Bown learned to knit from her grandmother at the ripe old age of six, so the simple forms of the sea urchins weren't much of a trial to her crafting skills. The biggest challenge? "Working to the deadline," says Bown, who, unlike many fiber artists these days, doesn't contract her work out but completes it all on her own. And without devising a pattern. She explains, "I want my work to be spontaneous and individual. I love experimenting, and it's quite exciting to watch work developing, as I don't know what will come out."

WOOLLY HAT
CAMPAIGN 2010

LANDS' END AND SAILORS' SOCIETY

Yargh, Nautical Toppers!

In autumn of 2009, catalog clothing retailer Lands' End sent out a curious call to its customers: Fifteen hundred woolly hats were needed by merchant seafarers. Would volunteer knitters take to their needles and stitch 'em up? The answer, of course, was an unequivocal yes, with knitters the world over writing in for kits containing Lands' End "feelgood yarn;" a pattern; a prepaid envelope for sending the completed hat to Sailors' Society, the charitable organization that has run the Woolly Hat Campaign since 2006; and a gift tag for adding a personalized message to a sailor.

No doubt, knitters were goaded to action by descriptions of the seafarers' way of life—not a romantic adventure, but a lifestyle fraught with discomfort and danger. As the photo below proves, it only takes a little knitting to make a whole lot of someones very happy indeed.

These happy seamen are the beneficiaries of Lands' End's Woolly Hat Campaign.
Photo by Sailors' Society

Things In, About, and From Nature

A knitted rose by any other name would still smell … like wool.

THE KNITTED LANDSCAPE

JAN TER HEIDE AND EVELEIN VERKERK

I Spy … Yarn!

The Knitted Landscape is an ongoing conceptual project that is the brainchild of Dutch artists Jan ter Heide and Evelein Verkerk. When they began work on it in 2006, their primary purpose "was to produce something soft and positive as a reaction to all the bad things happening around the world," they explain. And what resulted were knitted objects—mushrooms, flowers, stones, leaves, olives, more than one hundred of them—left in various locations around the world. The objects were then photographed, and the photographs eventually formed the core of an exhibition in which various landscapes were mimicked—there were trees, and yarn "waterfalls," and piles of actual rocks set up throughout the space, on which the knitted objects were placed—then the photographs hung among them, showing the objects as they appeared out in "the wild."

Curiously, the exhibition was not the end of *The Knitted Landscape* project. The artists maintain a website where dozens of other knitters continue to send photographs of their own objects set amid buildings and forests. "It's exciting to see how it grows," say ter Heide and Verkerk. Almost like a real flower.

You never know where they'll pop up: mushrooms at the monastery of Badia di Passignano, Tuscany; tucked into a hollow tree on London's Rochester Row; or in Arezzo, Italy, on the outer wall of the Piazzale del Campanile. *All items knitted and photographed by Jan ter Heide and Evelein Verkerk for Knitted Landscape*

Rock crops across Ireland, from top to bottom: Kylemore Lough in Connemara; The Burren, County Clare; and Cleggan Bay and Glassilaun Beach, Galway. *All items knitted and photographed by Jan ter Heide and Evelein Verkerk for Knitted Landscape*

THE KNITTED LANDSCAPE

IN THEIR OWN WORDS

Jan was going to Ireland and Evelien was going to France when we had the idea of knitting an object and leaving it at a beautiful spot for somebody to find. After that, the idea evolved into knitting flowers, mushrooms, etc. It was clear from the beginning that the idea was to make people laugh, or at least smile, when encountering one of our objects. We were also influenced by the random acts of kindness movement and the mood of the French film *Le fabuleux destin d'Amélie Poulin* (released in the United States as *Amélie*). The photo itself is the actual artwork.

Photo by Astrid van Loo, Deventer, the Netherlands

Leaving knitted objects and taking photographs gives you a real kick, the fantasy of someone finding it. If you find an object, the label attached to it directs you to the website. Here you can find out you're part of a worldwide art project. The label also says 'Knitted with Love,' which makes it a special personal gift. We've had some very nice e-mails from people who found one of our knitted objects. It doesn't happen with every object, but if we get a reaction, it's always positive.

We used brightly colored yarn to highlight the contrast with the surroundings. In a way, the presence of an alien object, such as a knitting-covered stone, changes the way you look at the landscape—this was a surprise to us. And the object also carries a memory of the landscape for the person who finds it. There is a contrast between the knitting, used mostly for practical things like socks and sweaters, and the rough, natural landscape. The handmade feeling of the knitted items, plus the idea that someone is crazy enough to spend 'valuable' time to make such things, gives something extra to these pieces of knitting.

Top: A rock cozy at Claggan Head, Galway, Ireland, with Knitted Landscape's signature tag. Middle: A knitted mushroom at the Temple of Janus in Autun, France. Bottom: In the fields of Cicmany, Slovakia. *All items knitted and photographed by Jan ter Heide and Evelein Verkerk for Knitted Landscape, except Cicmany, Slovakia; photograph by Rasto Meliska*

58

CITY OF STITCHES

ISABEL BERGLUND

Tree Hugger Extraordinaire!

Inspired by Paul Auster's book *City of Glass*, Isabel Bergland's 13-foot-tall walk-in creation from 2004 is stitched up of cotton yarn—a cozy city (of sorts) rather than a cool and brittle one. Viewers (or are they citizens?) are invited to enter, then "jump into the wall," as Berglund describes it. To do this, they put on a vest, or a skirt, or another one of the garments that Berglund has knitted then stitched right into the structure. Thus swaddled (or held prisoner, depending on one's perspective and attendant level of claustrophobia), they can ponder the lovely, loopy tree that looms at the center of the room.

To make such a city was not without its difficulties. For starters, Berglund knitted the entire structure by hand, from twenty strands of yarn manipulated into shape on size 19 (15mm) needles. The walls were sewn to metal poles that are then hung from the ceiling in whatever room the city is installed in—most recently, one at the Korean Craft

In Berglund's *City of Stitches*, a knitted tree grows in the middle of a knitted dome, which contains knitted garments to hold a captive audience—or an audience captive. *Photos by Christoffer Askman*

Biennale. It was difficult to get the walls "the right weight to hang," recalls Berglund.

Odd as *City of Stitches* may look in a photograph, in person its tactile charms are manifest. "The knitted walls isolate noise, like snow," says Berglund. "The audience feels like children: playing, laughing, and having fun."

If only all knitting could inspire such revelry.

59

KNIT KNOT TREE

NANCY MELLON AND
CORRINE BAYRAKTAROGLU

Keeping Your Favorite Tree
Warm This Winter!

Sometimes what's relevant about the act of knitting is not so much fancy stitches and complicated patterns, as the bringing together of people. That was certainly the case with the *Knit Knot Tree*, assembled in 2007 and 2008 in the town of Yellow Springs, Ohio. Its originators, artists Nancy Mellon and Corrine Bayraktaroglu, had planned merely to yarn-bomb a pear tree outside the community's Art Council headquarters in honor of its biannual Art Stroll Event. (For more on yarn bombing, see the Profile on KnittaPlease, page 90.) "It was a gray and gloomy winter, and seeing a cheerful tree in a sweater made people laugh," recalls Bayraktaroglu. But that was just the beginning of the enormous response the tree was to engender.

As Mellon and Bayraktaroglu assembled knit squares onto the trunk and limbs of the tree, "more advanced knitters literally stopped their cars with beautiful, complicated knitting hanging from their needles and asked if they could contribute. We sent them into the coffee shop to cast off, then helped them attach it right then and there," says Bayraktaroglu. Some of the squares were outfitted with pockets, and people left "all sorts of things in them: poems, pictures, jokes, candy, notes, little stuffed animals, coins, knitted socks, handmade beads, a stick of incense. One Saint Patrick's Day, there was an unopened can of beer in one of them."

By the time the knitting was cut from the tree, five months after it had begun to appear there, untold numbers of knitters had contributed to *Knit Knot Tree* and "officially, *lots*" of yarn had been used in its creation. But the way in which the tree brought the community together—despite some public concern that the knitting was injuring the tree (it wasn't) and that there were more constructive ways to use one's knitting needles—is the lingering message behind the project. According to Bayraktaroglu:

> The whole community seemed to become involved,
> from children and teenagers, to young adults and

oldsters. We also had people from out of town who, upon hearing about it from friends or relatives, visited the town just to put something on the tree. Children became curious about what sort of tree it was, and some of them were inspired to learn to knit. It inspired an online poetry contest. A couple 'tied the knot' under the tree. It also inspired discussions about recycling, but most of all it became a rallying point for the community, which enjoyed seeing what new gifts had been left on its branches [every day]. It showed up [in newspapers] around the world: China and Germany and so many places. We even had some people move to our town because of the *Knit Knot Tree*. They saw an article about it and thought any town willing to have something like this in their downtown was one they would want to live in. And they were right. It's a wonderful, magical town.

The Tree, snug in its multiarmed sweater. *Photo by Corrine Bayraktaroglu and Nancy Mellon*

60

THE KNIT GARDEN

TATYANA YANISHEVSKY

Flowers a Brobdingnagian Could Love!

Tatyana Yanishevsky conceived of this enormous, majestic garden for her senior thesis project at Brown University. It was, claims the self-taught knitter who didn't pick up needles till age eighteen, "the project that really taught me everything I know about knitting. It was sort of a high-stakes situation, where I was committed to my vision of knitted flowers and had to acquire the necessary knitting aptitude to make it happen.

"The earlier pieces were meant to be purely illustrative," she says. "They are anatomically correct models of plants I was fascinated by, plants that I was studying, working with, or happened to have in my house. I saw these pieces as absurd educational tools or toys for plant enthusiasts and scientists. I was interested in illustrating the tiniest of floral parts and magnifying these details to confront the

viewer with their bizarre allure. The minutia of flora so often goes unnoticed, though we all know flowers to be beautiful. By rendering them on such a large scale—oftentimes a larger-than-human scale—I was hoping to call attention to plants in a unique way. I was hoping to foster an unconventional interaction between plant and human and perhaps inspire some awe over the natural beauty that exists in this world."

Some of Yanishevsky's botanical delights, in the wild, and in the gallery.

Opposite page, top: *Anatomically Correct Passionflower.* Bottom: *Japanese Waterlily.*

This page, left: *Anatomically Correct Hibiscus.* Below: detail of a rotted rosehip berry from the piece *Rosehip Decay: From Falling Petal to Rotting Berry.*

Photos © 2009 Tatyana Yanishevsky

Profile

I taught myself how to knit when I was eighteen. I can't remember the specific impetus or the particular desire to start, but one day I started teaching myself how to knit using the Internet. I found it funny that I was learning such an old craft from the Internet and not, say, my grandmother.

I have a B.A. in biology and a B.A. in visual arts from Brown University. *The Knit Garden* began as my senior thesis. I was taking the plant systematic class (plant systematics refers to the biological classification of plants, often based on the plant's physical features, as well as lineage) and was endlessly intrigued with the minute, alien forms of plants. This was around the time I was learning to knit and developing a desire to create knitted forms that were fantastical and not necessarily functional. At some point, there was a collapsing of worlds and ideas, and the thought, 'Wouldn't it be amazing if there was a giant knit flower in the corner over there?' crossed my mind.

I became obsessed with all the different patterns that are possible in knitting. Knitting starts with such simplicity, but the combinations and patterns that arise are diverse and endless. I could pair and juxtapose stitches that created thick and dense fabrics, holey patterns that create lacy knits, cables, bobbles, and colored patterns. I found a book called *A Treasury of Knitting Patterns* by Barbara G. Walker, which is sort of an encyclopedia of stitch patterns. I've had it for years now and consult it whenever I need ideas or inspiration about what stitches to use. The overall form of the knit plant is a pattern that I make up based on the anatomy and shape of the actual plant. As far as I know, there are no published patterns on how to knit floral sculptural forms.

My earlier pieces involved a lot of math and precise calculations, test swatches for the patterns, and a lot of planning. At some point, my knitting practice became strong enough that I could just make up the pattern as I went along. I would give myself parameters, such as, 'This piece will increase evenly for about 1½ feet, and then it will be straight for 3 feet; it will have parallel veins, which will be represented by cable stitching; it will have bobbles in black yarn placed randomly between the veins; and random color patches to give variation to the yellow hue.' Or, 'This piece needs to have a pattern that is readable from both sides, and will have six veins, and because this isn't

Tatyana Yanishevsky with one of her flowers.

stuffed, it can be lacy and holey.' Then I'd allow myself room to play within those rules.

The process of knitting, stitch by stitch, mimics the growth of a plant, cell by cell. Unlike human development, a plant's growth is relatively simple: Cells grow forward from the meristem (a mass of undifferentiated cells). Each cell develops into the tissue where it ends up. There are no stem cells or zones of cells that are set to grow into specific tissue. The process of my knitting plants copies this natural process. In essence, I am growing my own plants, which are larger and slightly crazier than their naturally occurring counterparts. I also love that knitting does not lie. It's a direct, singular, additive process that one can decipher by studying the knitted fabric. I mean this in opposition to multilayered and multiphase processes such as mold making and casting from molds, blacksmithing and certain other kinds of metalworking, and printmaking. By additive, I mean in opposition to a subtractive process like wood carving.

continued

I weld steel to create the internal structures that I seek. I use PVC piping on occasion and have become quite fond of using cement at the base of a piece. There's usually pillow stuffing involved somewhere.

While my earlier work was primarily about the knitting and less about the other components, I have recently begun to expose other materials that I use. Exposing the metal, using dyed and yarn-embedded cement as its own element in the work, and bringing in resin and lighting allow me to explore relationships between knit yarn and these other materials—to play with their differences and similarities. Can I make all these diverse materials make sense together? Can I make my metalwork as textured as the knitting? Can I accentuate the differences between plastic and wool? Or, perhaps more interestingly, can I make them appear the same? These are the questions I've been asking myself as of late.

I think there's an easy entry point into *The Knit Garden* because we all have a familiar relationship with both knitted fabric and flowers. We all know someone who knits, we all know someone who gardens; we've all worn sweaters and seen flowers. I would like this easiness to be present only in the entrance to the body of work. I wonder about how to move in a more uncomfortable direction, to be more expressive, to incorporate more narrative, and to delve into darker issues and darker spaces in the context of the hand-knit, the soft, and the comforting.

Out of college I got a job working as a fisheries observer in Alaska. This is a seasonal field biology position. Basically, the Alaskan fisheries are managed by putting biologists on board commercial fishing vessels. We do stock assessment and transmit fishing data every day via satellite. It's pretty incredible, and it's the only fishery in the world managed in this way (live and in season). I did that four times over the course of three years, two winters and two summers. It's a three-month contract in which you live and work on various boats in the Bering Sea and the Gulf of Alaska. There was one winter where I worked on a catcher/processor vessel (factory on board, so we only had to go into port when the hull was full of product), and I spent about seventy-two hours on land in sixty days. While out fishing, there's always time to knit.

COCOONING

KELLY RIDLEY

Woman Hatches from Knitted Egg!

In January 2010, Ontario fiber artist Kelly Ridley set out to do literally what so many of us humans do only figuratively at various points in our lives: cocoon herself. Over the course of eight days, working for about five hours at a stretch, Ridley knit herself inside a giant egg as part of a local gallery exhibition. "I'm not claustrophobic, thank goodness," Ridley exclaims.

To begin, Ridley plunked herself in the gallery's front window. Then she cast on four stitches, and, using three size 11 (8mm) circular needles, she knit a round mat until it was large enough for her to sit on, then she started curving it up and out. "In the early and late stages, I had to physically turn myself around as I knit in a circle around myself," Ridley recalls. "During the middle stages, I was able to twist and knit over my shoulder, and of course, the further the

The cocoon progression: from halfway through to almost complete. *Kelly Ridley, Cocooning installation at ARTspace gallery, Chatham, Ontario, 2010*

The cocoon: Day Four. *Kelly Ridley, Cocooning installation at ARTspace gallery, Chatham, Ontario, 2010*

egg progressed, the more difficult it was to get in and out." Much of the yarn she used to make the cocoon was yarn she "unknit" from a web of a sock, a sweater, a hat, and a scarf, which were hanging nearby. Having to navigate around those threads only made Ridley's coming and going more difficult—the strands attaching the egg to the web had become structurally important.

Finally, after several days of intense knitting, the egg was a little over 3 feet high, and it encompassed Ridley completely. "It was very warm and soft, so being in there"— for about twenty minutes of completely sealed-off time—"was quite comfortable." Then Ridley cut a small steek at the egg's back and crawled out. "I had people sitting in the gallery just watching me knit, and people coming back every day to see the progress, and teenagers taking pictures with their cell phones. I found all this very exciting!" Kind of like an actual hatching. Only, says Ridley, "A lot less destructive!"

KNITTED CACTI

IRENE YORK

Cacti That Tickle Instead of Prickle!

Newly relocated to southern Arizona, former yarn shop owner Irene York found herself "captivated," she says, "by the variation in form, size, texture, and beauty of the cactus." So she set about knitting it. To date, she's stitched up dozens of woolly succulents, including interpretations of Fencepost, Old Man, and Yellow Barrel cacti, as well as many of her own imagining. "They're basically easy to knit," she admits. The only real challenge is experimenting with stitch patterns to "achieve the characteristics of a particular species." That, and "finding the perfect pot to display it in."

> ... Irene York found herself "captivated ... by the variation in form, size, texture, and beauty of the cactus."

A few of York's prickly specimens. *Photo by Irene York*

Which are real and which are yarn? *Photos by Irene York*

Knits of War (and Peace)

About as far as you can get from grannies knitting socks, but a prescient parody of knitting for the troops, is knitting up the tools of war—more often than not, a cry for its polar opposite.

PINK M.24 CHAFFEE

MARIANNE JORGENSEN

What All the Chic Tanks Will Be Wearing This Season!

A real, live combat tank from World War II (borrowed, after much negotiating, from the Danish government) forms the heart of *Pink M.24 Chaffee* by artist Marianne Jorgensen—a protest against the war in Iraq. In all, 3,500 swatches about 6 inches (15 centimeters) square were donated by more than one thousand contributors and stitched over the tank from its canon to its caterpillar tracks.

The tank was exhibited in April 2006 in front of the Nikolaj Contemporary Art Center in Copenhagen. Says Jorgensen, "The physical and personal acknowledgment in all of those knitted patches was, when joined together, a powerful visualization of thoughtful, meaningful knitting." Five seamstresses patched the cover together on site, and the spectacle of it was, by all accounts, an "eye-catcher."

"I wonder how many Danes have actually seen a tank?" muses Jorgensen. Let alone a tank cradled in soft pink knitting.

A cozy for a tank: Jorgensen's *Pink M.24 Chaffee*. Photo by Barbara Katzin

LUVGUN

ANNA HRACHOVEC

Pistol d'Amour!

Luvgun is the invention of twenty-eight-year-old toy pattern designer Anna Hrachovec, for sale on her website, mochimochiland.com, to knit up yourself for the object of your hatred/affection.

The barrel of *Luvgun* holds three soft hearts, a design element that seems to win over most anyone with an objection to knitting up a weapon. "It's turned out to be one of my more popular patterns," says Hrachovec. "It's both edgy and lovable." She stitched the gun up in wool—"it just feels nice in my hands and gives toys a soft and friendly look."

The main challenge to the project: figuring out how to make the barrel. "I wanted it to be hollow, but I didn't want it to be floppy," explains Hrachovec. "I was really happy with the solution I came up with. After a bit of measuring and trial and error, I designed the gun as two flat pieces, with the stitches for the barrel sections picked up from the handle section. To finish, after sewing the two halves of the gun together, I folded several inches of barrel section inside itself to form the hollow part. Doubling the knitting over like this gave the gun a smooth opening at the end and also gave the barrel structure. It was also just the right size for the hearts to fit snugly inside."

If only all guns were so accommodating.

Hrachovec's *Luvgun* "shoots" bullets shaped like hearts. *Photo by Anna Hrachovec/ mochimochiland.com*

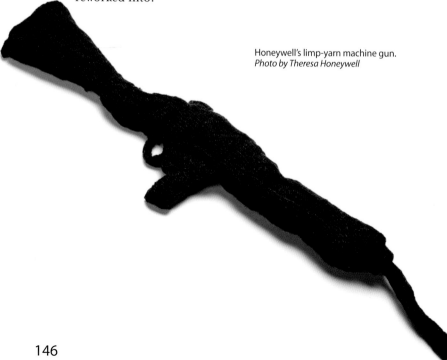

65
HAND KNIT MACHINE GUN

THERESA HONEYWELL

Now, Where Did I Put My Knitted Bullets?

If there's something a bit … flaccid about the appearance of Theresa Honeywell's *Hand Knit Machine Gun*, well, that's pretty much the point. In 2006, when she created this piece, Honeywell was in the throes of a divorce and feeling the need for empowerment. What better object than a machine gun to sum up all the frustrations of a marriage gone south? Says Honeywell, "It's a rigid and hard object in real life, but I have re-created it so that it loses its rigidity and falls limp in the hands of the viewer." So much metaphor, so little time …

While Honeywell's motorcycle cozy (see page 53) relies upon Red Heart acrylic yarn to achieve its particular sheen, the macho machine gun is made from soft and feminine wool and mohair. "I actually prefer nice yarns because they add symbolic meaning to the piece," says Honeywell. "It becomes more about the tactile quality of the material the yarn is reworked into."

Honeywell's limp-yarn machine gun.
Photo by Theresa Honeywell

88
STITCH FOR SENATE

CAT MAZZA

Calling All Senators!

In 2008, craftivist Cat Mazza sent a gift to every sitting U.S. senator. Well, in truth, it was less a gift than it was a political statement, about what she and thirty or so other knitters saw as the unfortunate nature of the continuing war in Iraq. One hundred helmet liners were stitched up and sent off in one hundred hand-knit pouches, some of them accompanied by personal statements by the men and women who did the knitting.

A helmet for Ohio Senator George Voinovich came with this comment by Heather Pristash: "As a lifelong Ohion who is also a liberal, I haven't agreed with Senator Voinovich about a great many things. However, I do believe that he cares about this country, even though he expresses his caring differently than I do." And this, for Senator Carl Levin of Connecticut, from Mike Topper: "This helmet liner is for our longtime senator, Carl Levin. A fixture on the Armed Services Committee as well as serving as the chair of that body more than once, he supports our men in service as well as anyone you can name. He did not support Joint Resolution 114, of which I am proud as he truly represented my vote." The point of all this? To encourage politicians to support the troops by bringing them home. To encourage them with *knitting*.

Knitting for the troops is nothing new. But Cat Mazza "wondered if I could do a seminal wartime initiative that supported the troops, but didn't support the war." Her project was supported by the organization Iraq Veterans Against the War, for which she also ran a veteran's scarf drive beginning in December 2008. It seemed a simple enough premise. Reactions among senators, though, were largely confused. "Thank you so much for thinking of me by sending a helmet liner. It was certainly thoughtful of you and I appreciate the warm gesture," wrote Orrin Hatch of Utah.

Knit your own Helmet Liner with the pattern on page 230!

Mazza's knitted helmet liners, ready to deploy to New York Senators Chuck Schumer and Hillary Clinton. *Photos by Cat Mazza*

87

BOMBOOZLE

MARIA PORGES

Finally—Softer, Safer Bombs!

In 2001, a lot happened to Maria Porges. She gave birth to twins in July. Then there were the events of September 11. "In all the hours I spent awake in the middle of the night," recalls Porges, "nursing and changing diapers and wondering just what I had been thinking when I got pregnant at age forty-six, since the world was apparently going to hell in a handbasket, I was trying to figure out what was going to come next."

She'd been at such a crossroads before, and usually, "I'd go back through all my notebooks, looking for clues" about what to do. This time was no exception. "I found some interesting stuff, including the narratives of a couple of significant dreams I had in the late nineties," she says. "One of them was about a woman who had been part of a radical cell of activists at college who had bombed a campus building. She had to go underground. Though this dream seemed to be more about what happens to lives that go in a direction that they were not meant to, the link to current events touched something off in me, and I read it over and over."

In the spring of 2002, Porges started making drawings from the story: "The wig the woman wore at her favorite professor's funeral, twenty-five years after the bombing, so she wouldn't be recognized," as Porges recalls it. There was also "a glass, sweating gently, full of some kind of hard liquor and ice, and bombs. I drew them as those cartoony forms that I knew from watching *Road Runner* on Saturday mornings—the silly spherical shape that the damn things always took in the *Mad Magazine* strip called 'Spy vs. Spy.'"

Eventually, she made most of those forms into sculpture, "but the bombs were first," she says. "I started out casting them in tinted beeswax, then tried terra cotta, glass, even bronze. But by far the most interesting version was the knitted, felted balls that I commissioned a woman named Louise to knit."

Porges purchased a sampling of yarn from three local yarn shops, but as "no one could really tell me which would felt best," she wound up with a number of textures in the finished pieces. "Sometimes within the same bomb, even," she marvels. "I drew patterns, designated which colors I wanted Louise to use together, how big I was thinking I wanted them to end up being—this was pretty hard to predict—and she set to work. She returned them to me every few weeks as limp little carcasses and strips of knitting. She figured out a way to knit the 'collar' through which the fuse emerges, and also the fuse itself." Porges herself sewed the collars, felted them and the bombs in the washing machine as many as four times, then stuffed and assembled each one, "twisting more yarn around each fat little fuse before sewing it in place. I used these felted fuses for another piece—three blown-glass bombs, called 'Bomb School'—and the contrast in textures is very nice."

The softest of all possible bombs: *Bomboozle* by Porges. *Photo courtesy of University of California, Berkeley Art Museum, and Pacific Archive. Gift of David Henry Jacobs*

The completed *Bomboozle*, consisting of fifty-nine bombs, was first shown in March 2003—the same month that President Bush was "putting us into a war that no one understood," says Porges. "Let's just say that this show, um, *bombed* commercially, though a lot of people liked its content. Eventually, I made another fifty or so bombs, and the final version of the piece, which belongs to the Berkeley Art Museum, has a total of ninety-nine bombs."

Porges describes the act of making the bombs "very, very enjoyable. In the end, they were everything I had imagined and more. Horrifyingly cute. Like land mines, one reviewer wrote ... the ones that kids pick up in former war zones, with disastrous results."

KNITNOTWAR 1,000

SEANN McKEEL

More Cranes Than You Can Shake a Stick At!

In 2007, while riding a bus (to the local yarn shop, no less) in her hometown of Portland, Oregon, Seann McKeel hit upon the idea that was to consume her for the next three years. "The people in front of me had been talking about the war [in Iraq]," she recalls. "A little while later I looked out the window and noticed a plastic bag fluttering in a tree that made me think of a crane. I immediately took a ball of yarn from my bag and started to compose a knit, origami-style crane."

Not, perhaps, the first impulse that would come to every knitter's mind. But McKeel had recently been living in Japan and visited the Children's Peace Monument in Hiroshima. Constructed in 1958, this bronze statue memorializes a young girl named Sadako Sasaki who, having been exposed to the bombing of Hiroshima, later contracted leukemia. She folded paper cranes until her death eight months later, believing that if she could fold one thousand of them, she would recover. Today, some ten million cranes have been left at the monument. And, McKeel hopes, her own contribution will soon join them.

Knit your own Crane with the pattern on page 231!

It's been slow going. After devising the pattern—"the knitting is really very simple! The biggest challenge is blocking and stitching it to get it to sit chin up, wings out, and tail up"—McKeel put out the call to her fellow knitters. But, "I had a baby with a husband who was on tour, and knitters would pledge to send then didn't, and then some would pledge to send ten and send one or two."

And so the knitting of cranes continued—and continued—with McKeel, even in her moments of doubt, still having no intention of cheating the numbers with a few paper versions. "I do enjoy folding paper origami; however, to say that I could even keep up with a folding fifth grader is a gross exaggeration," she quips. At last, in June 2010, McKeel had assembled all one thousand—just in time for an installation in the lobby of Ace Hotel Portland. Her mom helped considerably with the final fifty. "We rarely talk about her first husband, who died in Vietnam," remarks McKeel. "It's a really painful subject for her, but she managed to speak about it a bit while we were working on the cranes."

Throughout the years of the project, enthusiasm among crane knitters, whether they donated one or ten, remained high. "I just kept collecting one at a time," says McKeel, and the reaction "has been overwhelming. No one except interviewers even asks me why I'm doing it. People seem to intuit that the cranes are as much about personal hope as they are about peace."

A crane in the hand … is worth nearly 1,0o0 in the bush. *Photos by Seann McKeel Knitnotwar 1,0o0*

This is the original flyer that Seann distributed in 2007.

knitnotwar 1,0o0

An art installation, knitnotwar 1,0o0 is a project of peace.

The origami crane is an international symbol of peace, due to the hopeful and heroic story of Sadako Sasaki. Sadako died of leukemia after exposure from U.S. atom bombings of Hiroshima in 1945. Following a Japanese tradition of folding 1,000 paper cranes—a kind of prayer for long life and recovery—Sadako hoped to get well. She completed over 1,000 before dying in October 1955 at the age of twelve.

Artists will knit 1,000 origami-style cranes, which will be publicly displayed in late 2007 in Portland, Oregon.

* To help us reach the goal of 1,000 cranes, please pledge/submit 10 or more!

* Organize a group of ten knitters in your city and oversee the donation of 100!

Crane Deadline: May 1, 2007

Please complete the RSVP form on the back by March 1, 2007.

If you live in Portland, please visit www.knitnotwar.com for drop-off locations and save yourself the postage!

Need help with the pattern? Want to learn to knit? Desire more information or would like to get involved in the project?

Write Seann: knitnotwar@gmail.com.

RSVP

Name: _____

Address: _____

_____

Email: _____

Please RSVP/pledge your 10-crane donation by March 1, 2007. If you have others helping you knit your crane pledge, please be sure to include their names, addresses, and emails. Deadline for submission: May 1, 2007. Cranes from knitnotwar 1,0o0 are considered donations. Send your RSVP and cranes to 4725 N Mississippi Portland, Oregon 97217or RSVP at knitnotwar@gmail.com.

More information available soon at www.knitnotwar.com.

Scientifik

Who knew you could knit science? Well, the masterminds behind these entries, for starters. Could there be a knitted working robot in our future? We can only hope.

KNITTED MOLECULES

ANNE-MARIE DUNBAR

World's First Cuddly Chemicals!

Acetone (used to make nail polish), benzene (an industrial solvent), and ethanol (pure grain alcohol) might not seem to have much to do with crafty comforts. Unless these ordinarily highly flammable organic and chemical compounds are—you guessed it—knitted.

The three noxious liquids—along with the compound that makes acrylic yarn (acrylonitrile) and the one that makes you feel happy when you eat chocolate (theobromine)—were stitched up by thirty-seven-year-old Nottingham mum Anne-Marie Dunbar who, not surprisingly, has a background in organic and analytical chemistry. They're fashioned from acrylic yarn, "partly

Dunbar's happy organic chemistry family. *Photo by Anne-Marie Dunbar*

because it's machine washable and hardwearing, but also because it's easier to get a hold of bold colors in the UK in acrylic yarn, to match the colors used to represent the molecules," says Dunbar. Balls and sticks were knitted separately on double-pointed needles using a crocheted cast-on, then, after stuffing, all the elements (no pun intended) were seamed together "in the appropriate places, which would," muses Dunbar, "entail either some knowledge of molecular structure or a spot of googling."

Though the molecules are simple-looking enough, they actually present a variety of creative head-scratchers. Explains Dunbar: "I did have to give a lot of thought to gauge, and there was maths, and pi," in order to calculate the number of rows and stitches needed to create a 2-inch sphere. "The final stitching together is a challenge. Keeping the sticks

Top: acetone. Bottom: benzene. *Photos by Anne-Marie Dunbar*

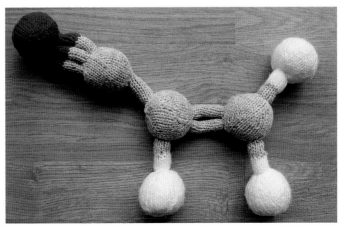

from twisting while you stitch—particularly on the double and triple bonds—could possibly challenge your sanity. Lots of pins at this point help. And placement of the sticks is important. The single bonds are quite straightforward at one end; generally, I just place them over the cast-off point. But then you have to put a bit of thought into where you want the ball at the other end to be attached, whereabouts the other bonds are going to be attached—that sort of thing."

Sounds an awful lot like ... *science*.

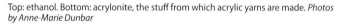

Top: ethanol. Bottom: acrylonite, the stuff from which acrylic yarns are made. *Photos by Anne-Marie Dunbar*

70

FROG AND RAT DISSECTIONS

EMILY STONEKING

World's First Adorable Biology Experiments!

What to do when you're downsized from your job in a stained glass studio? Readers of this book might be the first to clamor: start knitting! Only, Vermont resident Emily Stoneking took her knitting into a slightly …unusual realm, one that might elicit shudders from any gentle souls who feel they barely survived the grotesqueries of high school biology.

Stoneking knits dissections. Rats, frogs, fetal pigs. And while the real thing may once have sent some of us running and shrieking from the lab, the knitted versions are, dare it be said, downright adorable. "I get lots of [Etsy] orders," says Stoneking, "from people who are totally thrilled to have found the perfect gift for the researcher or biologist in their lives."

 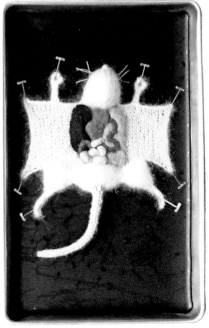

A biology experiment gone terribly wooly—Emily Stoneking's *Frog* "dissection."

She's not a biologist herself, but "I have a deep respect for science. I find bodies and their systems to be fascinating, and I particularly like art from the Age of Enlightenment that depicts the explorations of the human body." (Yes, she's working on some human body pieces, too. Stay tuned.) Unsurprisingly, her projects entail quite a lot of research, which includes studying dissection images. Then, "I begin knitting with a particular shape in mind, ripping out and starting again if I'm not getting the result I want." For the insides of the unfortunate animals in her slightly grisly menagerie, Stoneking uses needle felting and has taken certain "artistic liberties with the guts, instead of making them totally accurate in terms of coloring and placement."

"I get lots of [Etsy] orders from people who are totally thrilled to have found the perfect gift for the researcher or biologist in their lives."

To date, Stoneking has sold about two hundred of her flayed critters, including one that will find a permanent home in the National Museum of Health and Medicine. Virtually visit the museum at nmhm.washingtondc.museum.

KNITMINDER APP

PAUL MIETZ EGLI

Keep Track of Your Knitting!
With Technology!

One thing's for sure—this is not the tool your knitting granny has been waiting to get ahold of. But for a growing and increasingly excited populace, the KnitMinder app for the iPhone and iPod touch is the *only* way to keep track of everything knit related, from yarn stash and needles to what row and stitch you left off on with your latest UFO (or ten). And all for "less than the price of a fancy coffee!" carps the description on the Quilt2Go website, where KnitMinder lurks.

It's the brainchild of Santa Cruz, California, app designer Paul Mietz Egli, who designed his first freelance crafting app when his wife, Heather, exasperated with his continual ravings about the then-brand new iPhone, asked, "Can it organize my quilting fabric stash?" Mietz Egli's answer: "You know, it probably could." The later KnitMinder app was similarly inspired by Heather. Says Mietz Egli, "She knows exactly how it feels to come home from the yarn shop and realize that you've just purchased your fourth set of size eight circular needles. I knew the abilities of the iPhone inside and out. So we make a very effective team."

To the delight of anyone who's purchased KnitMinder, the price of purchase ($2.99) comes with hands-on help from Mietz Egli himself. "KnitMinder users can contact me directly from within the application, and I answer all e-mails personally," he says. "I also track every feature request or problem and incorporate user suggestions into each update of the application."

So what's the future of technology in knitting? According to Mietz Egli, "A phone that is always connected to the Internet and has a camera, giv[ing] you the ability to share a visual record of what you are doing with your knitting circle. Devices with a large amount of storage can remember things that you can't, like whether you have enough skeins of a particular yarn to complete a pattern you are considering at the local yarn shop." All of which may give tech-unsavvy grannies a bit of pause.

INVADER SCARF

What Is Your Knitwear Trying to Tell You?

Imagine this: You are walking down the street, minding your own business, when a complete stranger runs up and scans your scarf with an iPhone. The action of a lunatic? No, just the over-ebullience of a craft-techie who's gotten wind of the collaborative scarves made by London-based pixel knitwear designers, Office Lendorff, and Swiss "mobile enthusiasts," Kaywa.

The *Invader Scarves* are, as their name suggests, a series of limited-edition scarves that use Space Invaders as inspiration for a stitch pattern. "We love the old-school computer games," says designer Uschi Lescher, a former Austrian women's snowboard champion who runs Office Lendorff with her husband, Georg Lendorff. "You will find that most of our scarves are somehow inspired by computer games." The pattern itself was worked out old-school, too, on a piece of graph paper. "Once I have the basic idea, I translate it to the computer and basically design pixel by pixel. One pixel is like one stitch," says Lescher. The final scarves were knit up by a manufacturer in the north of England.

But not before a secret message had been decided upon, which the manufacturer embeds into the body of the knitting. To read it (there are two versions of the message, actually, neither of which Lescher will divulge), you simply download a free QR code reader from Kaywa onto your mobile phone, scan the code with it (bottom right end in the photo, just above "Lendorff.Kaywa") and voilà! Message decoded.

The code is more than just a gimmick, though. It's a way for Office Lendorff to produce a "small, exclusive collection" that most people can afford. "Design and genuineness should make a product affordable," maintains the design duo. "Not price."

Lendorff.Kaywa's knitted scarf,
which reveals a hidden message
when scanned with your iPhone.
Photo by Lendorff.Kawywa

73

THE BIG MICROBE KNIT

CLARE DYER-SMITH

Pardon Me, Madam, but Is Your Knitting Contagious?

As is evident from the photo, there's nothing especially complicated about knitting cholera. But organizers of the 2009 Manchester (UK) Science Festival approached physics doctoral candidate Clare Dyer-Smith to run a workshop at the event on knitting microbes, with only one important idea in mind: to teach folks about germs.

It was a project the twenty-six-year-old Portsmouth, UK, native embraced with a sort of giddy, science-geek aplomb. "I enjoyed knitting the salmonella the most," she says. Not a pronouncement you hear every day from knitters you know.

What's so great about knitted microbes? They're guaranteed *not* to make you sick.

Cholera (top) and the common cold (bottom), in decidedly non-illness-bearing form.
All photos by Clare Dyer-Smith © 2009

In all, Dyer-Smith designed and stitched up six microbes: tuberculosis, cholera, salmonella, rhinovirus (also known as the common cold), swine flu, and penicillium, which is the fungus penicillin is made of. "The idea was to keep the patterns simple and also to use them to highlight some of the specific features of microbes," recalls Dyer-Smith, "such as the flagella that bacteria use to move, and the proteins that viruses use in order to get into cells."

Knit your own Swine Flu Microbe with the pattern on page 233!

To continue such educational efforts, all the microbes knit at the event were collected at the day's end and distributed, and Dyer-Smith posted all the patterns as free downloads on her Ravelry page: www.ravelry.com/patterns/library/microbes.

The affair engendered some unexpected results. "People were using their imaginations and making completely new microbes," recalls Dyer-Smith. "One man crocheted methicillin-resistant staphylococcus aureus bacteria using fine yellow yarn." Yes, but as any six-year-old would like to know, will a stash of knitted staph bacteria pack enough punch keep you home sick from school?

Salmonella (top) and tuberculosis (bottom), in decidedly nonthreatening form.
Photos by Clare Dyer-Smith © 2009

Do the Math

Every knitter has had to contend with a little bit of math at some point. But this math is something else entirely.

74

MATHEMATICAL AFGHANS

WOOLLY THOUGHTS, PAT ASHFORTH AND STEVE PLUMMER

Extremely Math-y!

If only we'd all had math teachers like the Ashforth–Plummers growing up, our educations would have been considerably more colorful, to say the very least. And perhaps a lot more explicable, too. Knitted afghans representing things like the binary system and multiplication tables may not seem particularly useful on first consideration. But hearing Steve Plummer's story about exhibiting one such afghan at a UK math fair in 1997 helps crystallize the afghans' quiet relevancy.

Remembers Plummer, "Partway through the day, a girl, aged thirteen, wandered in alone and was instantly drawn to *Counting Pane*"—an afghan that represents the number 1–10 on the first row, 11–20 on the second, and so on. Each number is color-coded, and each square also contains colors representing what numbers it is divisible by. "We asked her a few questions about *Counting Pane*, and she became more and more involved and more and more animated. Her answers were extremely

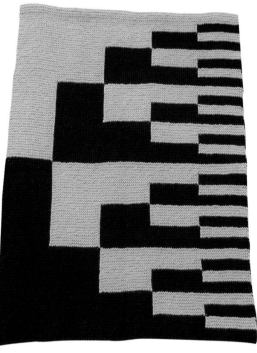

Double Base represents the binary system's Base 2 counting system, prevalent in building computers and electronic equipment. *Photo by Pat Ashforth and Steve Plummer www. woollythoughts.com*

perceptive, and she talked at great length and in great depth about the patterns she was seeing. Her responses suggested that she had a very logical train of thought and a thorough understanding of concepts behind what we were asking her. We were shocked when she told us she was 'useless in maths.' During the afternoon she returned with a succession of friends, and toward the end of the day reappeared yet again with her maths teacher. She didn't ask him any questions, but proceeded to lecture him with her newfound confidence in her own ability. He was astounded. We like to think *Counting Pane* may have had a lasting effect on that girl—and her teacher."

What this little story affirmed for Ashford and Plummer was quite significant, all the more so considering that the two are secondary school math teachers who have the opportunity to test their ideas in the classroom: Not everyone sees things in the same way; some people have a

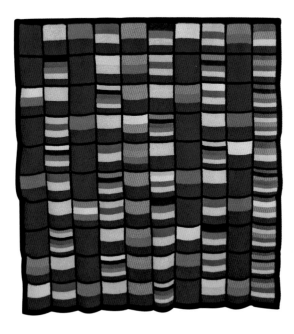

Arguably Woolly Thoughts' most "important" afghan, *Counting Pane*, consists of 100 squares in 10 rows, the first row represents the numbers 1–10; the second, 11–20 and so forth. Colors represent factors: Blue for 1, yellow for 2, red for 3, green for 4, raspberry for 5, brown for 6, pink for 7, pale blue for 8, orange for 9, and purple for 10. But the intrigue runs even deeper than that. *Photo by Pat Ashforth and Steve Plummer www.woollythoughts.com*

much more visual approach than others; math does not have to be about writing things down; students may have a very distorted view of their own capabilities; and some pupils need unconventional triggers to begin the thought process.

Sign us up—we're ready to go back to math class!

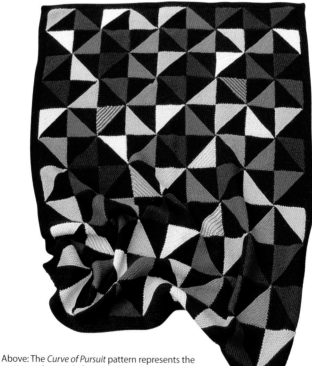

Above: The *Curve of Pursuit* pattern represents the equi-angular spirals formed when "four dogs set off to chase each other from the corners of a field," says Plummer. The curves become more obvious as points along the route are connected. *Photo by Pat Ashforth and Steve Plummer www.woollythoughts.com*

Below: The *Tilting at Windmills* afghan poses the question: What makes a pattern? According to Plummer, viewers strongly disagree as to whether or not a pattern is in effect here. *Photo by Pat Ashforth and Steve Plummer www.woollythoughts.com*

75

PIXELATED SWEATERS

JIM DRAIN

Sweaters to Boggle Your Brain!

Atari lovers, these knits are for you: twenty-nine one-off sweaters by Jim Drain, the big daddy of knitted sculpture, featuring takes on some of those bright screen graphics you once knew so well down at the arcade. (Maybe you can even call to memory some of Drain's own favorite vids: "Double Dragon Kung Fu" and "The Legend of Zelda"?)

The sweaters riff on the idea that "knitting and weaving can be seen as utilizing the first computer language, in that within

Jim Drain's sweater of hearts … hearts … hearts … *Photo courtesy Greene Naftali Gallery*

a garment or rug, etc., is the 'code,'" the Miami-based Drain told *T Magazine*. He constructed his garments on a Stoll industrial knitting machine at the Rhode Island School of Design starting in the summer of 2009, inspired by the machine's capabilities. "It was interesting to find the limits of the machine," Drain remarks. "There are things that can't be done with either a hand knitting machine nor a manual knitting machine (and vice-versa). It offered a new way to look at knitting and how the machine itself informed the patterning decisions."

While the look of the things—boxy-shaped and replete with oversaturated repeats of hearts and bricks—may seem to hark back to the 1980s, the feel of them certainly doesn't. They're soft "like butter," thanks to JaggerSpun merino from Maine. While Drain admits it would have been cheaper to stitch up the knits using acrylic yarn, and that such material allows for some pretty "saturated" colors, "After three hours of having a sweater on your body, there's something so nice about natural wool." Hear, hear! It's a sentiment the sweaters' buyers, as winter approaches, will no doubt be grateful for.

A ninja busts through a knitted brick wall in Drain's brick sweater. *Photo courtesy Greene Naftali Gallery*

78

TWO-PATTERN DOUBLE KNITTING

ALASDAIR POST-QUINN

It's One Thing! *And* Another!

There's double knitting (see M'Lou Baber's *Cat Coat*, page 83). Then there's what Massachusetts native Alasdair Post-Quinn does. Call it "Extreme Double Knitting," because, simply, it is.

Where your average color-patterned double knitting results in a piece of fabric that has a flower motif in blue, say, on one side and white on the other, two-pattern double knitting such as what Post-Quinn accomplishes might feature a pattern of flowers on one side, and of birds on the other. No tricks. No gimmicks. No two pieces of differently patterned fabric stitched together. Just a lot of experimentation. And a brand-new system of charting, invented by Post-Quinn himself.

He doesn't take the credit for inventing two-pattern double knitting, though. "It was an

Post-Quinn's *Falling Blocks Hat* features a different pattern on either side. *Photos courtesy of www.fallingblox.com*

accident by one of my students at one of the earliest double-knitting workshops I taught," he recalls. "The student had correctly moved the yarn ends so there were no bars, but one particular stitch was the same color on one side as it was on the other. She pulled it out and fixed it, but it got me thinking." One of the things Post-Quinn got thinking about was how to solve the ages-old irritation of double-knitters everywhere: what to do about letters. As Post-Quinn explains it: "If you double knit a letter, the opposite side will be reversed in color but also reversed in orientation. The result is a mirror image letter on the opposite side, which makes the whole reversibility element of your work a little less effective." But if you can knit a separate pattern on the reverse side, problem solved.

Of course, the question plaguing the uninitiated is "*How on Earth does he do it?* And luckily, Post-Quinn will be writing the book on the subject, to be published by "Knit Girl" Shannon Okey. In brief, and of course, all in Post-Quinn's words, because pretty much no one else in the world is qualified to explain it. Here goes:

"Double knitting has rules, like any other technique. Some can be bent in interesting ways. Rule number one for double-knitting colorwork is that if you use color A on the front, you will use color B on the back. This way, you can knit a pattern using only a standard chart, and mentally insert the opposite color purl after each knit stitch you make." You with him so far?

"But what if you use color A on the front and then use the same color A on the back? You have a strand, an unused color running between the stitches, but it opens up more possibilities." Such as Falling Blocks on one side of a hat, and a looped chain on the other. Says Post-Quinn, "I determined that it is actually better if the two patterns are radically different from each other. The more chaos, the more stable the fabric. You want the colors to change as much as possible—above all, you don't want to have large expanses where the work is the same color on both sides, and then you will see the strand when the work is stretched."

He charts such dual patterning with a system of his own devising, a stitch-by-stitch notation method that he calls "almost completely unintelligible—the first one I did looked like a crossword puzzle on hallucinogens." More helpfully he offers, "Essentially, you take two charts, mirror-image the one that will be on the back, then separate each column by the width of another column. Interlace the two patterns so the first column is from the front pattern and the last column is from the back column. Overlay the back pattern columns with purl dots and leave the front pattern columns plain, and you have a two-pattern notation chart." *Now* are you still with him?

Believe it or not, reading and writing his own charts are not the greatest hurdle to Post-Quinn's knitting. The prototyping is. "I have an idea, I see how it will come together, and I start knitting it. It's disheartening to find that something that was such a perfect solution in your mind doesn't work as elegantly in real life. But every design is a learning process for me." So much so that he's already got solutions worked out for the next version of his Falling Blocks hat, which irks him because he finds the amount of same-color space in the center of each pattern repeat to be too large. He'll get that worked out in the next prototype. How? Don't get him started …

Post-Quinn's *Victorian Raffia Scarf*: Just your average, run-of-the-mill double knitting. *Photos courtesy of www.fallingblox.com*

77

KNITTED FRACTALS

ELEANOR KENT

Groovy!

Though she doesn't have a background in math, San Francisco native Eleanor Kent found that she was "fascinated by the wonderful fractal designs that can be seen now that computers can do calculations to make them visible." In the blink of an eye, she went from using color Xerox machines to reproduce her work to send it out as Mail Art to other artists, to drawing with the computers that were coming out in the 1980s. Says Kent, "I got an Apple IIe with a color monitor that had large pixels that looked like knitted stitches. I liked the fabulous computer-generated designs I saw on monitors and in books and wanted to understand them more. So I xeroxed them and graphed them on graph paper.

Then I knitted them." To do this, Kent collaborated with other artists and mathematicians, who could make patterns on paper for her to follow.

To achieve her desired results, Kent chose two colors she liked and worked in what she terms "the Fair Isle style, carrying the yarn in back." She mostly uses single-strand worsted weight yarn and size 10 (6mm) needles, and when the pieces are complete, she sews cloth tape to one end and hangs them on the wall, or makes them into baby blankets or scarves.

Explains Kent, "Fractals are mathematical figures that are self-similar; each part is like each other part on all size levels, and they are one-and-a-half dimensions. I liked the correspondence between pixel and stitch, but computer graphics are not very tactile. I wanted to make things that I could touch." Sound like any other knitters you know?

The yarny algorithms of Kent: *Sign of Juno* (1996), opposite; *Binary Decomposition* (1988), top; and *Inglesia Rosa* (1994), bottom. *All photos © Eleanor Kent 2009*

78

HYPERBOLIC PLANES

DAINA TAIMINA

Cool Math They Never Told You About in High School!

There's been a lot of attention paid in the past couple of years to the Institute for Figuring's crocheted coral reef—which has engendered all sorts of wacky yarn craftivism the globe over. Suddenly, every fiber artist and his mother is crocheting impossibly frilled sea forms and other fantastical constructions. And it's all thanks to one woman: a Cornell University mathematics researcher named Daina Taimina.

In 1997, Taimina figured out how to use yarn and hook to create the first tactile model depicting a concept called the hyperbolic plane. The hyperbolic plane is an idea discovered in the mid-nineteenth century that proposes a surface made up of space that is constantly curving away from itself—unlike a sphere, which constantly curves in on itself to create a closed space. Basically, such a form looks like ruffles, and ruffles on ruffles. It's not an idea that can be proved with formulae, so the only way to represent a hyperbolic plane is

The Day and The Night in Hyperbolic Space (2007) measures 18 inches × 18 inches × 16 inches (46cm × 46cm × 40cm) and was created using two colors of wool changing equally, from one skein of turquoise, to one skein of dark blue, and back again. Its weight is approximately 6 pounds (3kg), and uses fifteen skeins of each color. "I was expecting it to be more chaotic, but that did not happen," says Taimina. "Instead, the colors kind of split apart—one side took more turquoise, the other more blue, therefore the title *The Day and The Night*." *Artist/photo © Daina Taimina*

The Land and The Sea, 2009, 19½ inches × 19½ inches × 8 inches (50cm × 50cm × 20cm), mixed yarn, was made for the Latvian project *From Coral Reefs to Baltic Sea*, meant in part to raise awareness about the dying Baltic Sea. In all, 643 crocheters participated. Recalls Taimina: "My most emotional experience with the project was meeting some young people with psychological and learning disabilities who contributed to this project, and also learning that [it] helped people in remote villages come together and help each other during the economic crisis—doing crochet together opened them up to talk about their problems." *Artist/photo © Daina Taimina*

with a model—and this was not satisfactorily achieved until the late 1970s, with various tape and paper constructions that were difficult to assemble and delicate to handle.

Latvian-born Taimina began to use her girlhood craft skills to devise a solution, which her geometry-professor husband used for teaching. A year later, the two gave a talk about the models to a group of math professors. "That second day, everyone had gone to Jo-Ann Fabrics, and had yarn and crochet hooks," Taimina told the *New York Times* in 2005. To this day, she receives an inordinate number of requests from geometry departments all over the world for her own incredible, handmade specimens.

The hyperbolic plane shows up in all sorts of places we take for granted—in some lettuce leaves and wood ear mushrooms, as well as kelp and coral. (Asked why mathematicians had never noticed before the 1800s that these shapes had nothing at all to do with planar geometry, Taimina's husband quipped to an interviewer for the journal *Cabinet*: "There are ... not that many mathematicians sitting around looking at sea slugs.") Taimina attempted to knit it first, but found that, since a hyperbolic plane increases exponentially, too many stitches had to be held on the knitting needles all at once to make for easy handling. Since "crocheting doesn't require all the stitches to be held on the needles simultaneously," explained a 2006 *Discover* magazine article, Taimina could use more stitches per inch. To whit: A sea anemone that begins with an inner row of stitches that is 1½ inches long, is 30 feet (or 369 inches) long 22 rows later.

So are crocheted hyperbolic planes math? Or art (Taimina's had scores of exhibits)? Both—and so much more. They can help computer animators figure out how to model skin, and help engineers to work with airflow. They also apply to tailoring: Taimina crocheted a hyperbolic skirt that used a mile and a half of yarn for its ruffles dividing into more ruffles, similar to a pattern for an old-fashioned godet skirt, which, she told *Discover*, "Is known to flatter any figure." Now that really is a happy marriage of art and science!

Global Warming, 2008, which measures 20 inches × 28 inches × 28 inches (72cm × 72cm × 50cm), nylon yarn, is the largest hyperbolic plane Taimina has crocheted to date, and it took her eight months to complete it. The pink top is made from a piece of ribbon nearly 3½ miles long. *Artist/photo © Daina Taimina*

Metallurgy

No one would argue that these knits are soft and cuddly. They won't even keep you warm. And they're probably the only examples of knitting that will set off airport metal detectors.

79

LEAD TEDDY BEAR

DAVE COLE

Much, Much Heavier Than the Average Bear!

When is a teddy bear not a teddy bear? You could argue: When it loses any purported and cuddly functionality by being knit of lead into a critter so heavy no child could ever lift it. That's right, Dave Cole (see page 20) befuddles knitting grannies again, with his knitted series of dead-weight "toys" that defy conventional notions of playthings.

To knit these bears, he first had to construct the needles—out of solid steel, as traditional knitting needles would have shattered under the heft of lead. But for Cole, such preliminary construction work is part of the fun: "It's a meditative first step to get me creating in the studio," he says. "And I'm a total geek for tools." Not surprising, coming from a guy who learned to weld at age eleven, and spent a large chunk of his childhood hanging out in his grandfather's blacksmithing shop.

> Dave Cole befuddles knitting grannies again, with his knitted series of dead-weight "toys" that defy conventional notions of playthings.... "I can use anything and transform it."

Wearing supportive wrist braces, Cole stitched up the bears from lead ribbon he manipulated over steel armatures; then, he plumped them up with lead wool (cousin to steel wool) stuffing. Since "knitting is a technique rather than a medium," says Cole, "it allows access to all these different materials. I can use anything and transform it. I love taking material and working with it in a way that is [unexpected]."

And, most assuredly, a lead bear is nothing if not surprising. At least as surprising as another of Cole's knitted bears: a 14-foot-tall teddy made of fiberglass, for which he had to wear a full-body hazmat suit because "I was using my arms as knitting needles."

As for the challenges of knitting up such a ... hearty object, Cole says, "To work with lead, you've got to understand soft metals. Once you have that ability, then you can create an object. You can make lead look like leather!" Will lead be the "yarn" of the future?—after all, it's abundant, pliable, and won't melt till you heat it to 600°F. Not likely— it's also *poisonous*.

One of Cole's lovable lead teddy bears. *Photo courtesy of theknittingmachine.com and Judi Rotenberg Gallery*

80

STEEL WIRE FINGER KNITTING

BLANKA SPERKOVA

Real Wire—No Tricks!

While Dave Cole fashions special needles to knit his Lead Teddy Bears, Slovakian artist Blanka Sperkova uses nothing more than her own hands to form her wire sculptures. To do this, she uses a technique she calls "finger knitting," although, intriguingly, this owes less to the old-fashioned kid's craft than it does to another, almost lost art form.

"In the eighteenth and nineteenth centuries, poor people from northern Slovakia used to travel around Europe, repairing pots and ceramics," Sperkova explains. "They wired the broken pots together with nets—actually, this tradition is very alive in the last few years after the Velvet Revolution, and some tinkers use knitting also. I wanted to find out how these traditional tinkers did their work. But I discovered something rather different." Pushing a strand of steel wire through previously made loops of wire, Sperkova succeeded in creating a structure of netting that looked—and actually is, at its core of interlocking loops—knitted.

"I come from a region of Slovakia where lace making is still a traditional occupation for women," she maintains. And in truth, her sculptures—embryos floating in spheres, and undulating free-forms—for all the heft of the steel that composes them, are astonishingly lacy looking. In some instances, they appear no denser than the shadows they cast on their surrounding

Two of Sperkova's knitted wire objects: From left to right: *To Picasso* (2007), a necklace made of lacquered wire; and *Opened World* (2002), in all its shadowy beauty. *Photos courtesy of the artist*

walls. Says Sperkova, "The gauge of the wire determines the
size of the knitted loops, and that dictates the volume" of a
finished piece. "If I do not respect the dictates of structure,
the form loses its shape, its inner stress, its virtue."

Though Sperkova does not now indulge in the virtues
of knitting with softer stuff, she does remember knitting
clothing for herself, once upon a time, underneath her desk
at school ("only my math teacher discovered" the secret).
After a group show of her works at a gallery in Washington,
D.C., in 2005, Sperkova's knitted wire sculptures are,
happily, no longer a secret to American art-goers.

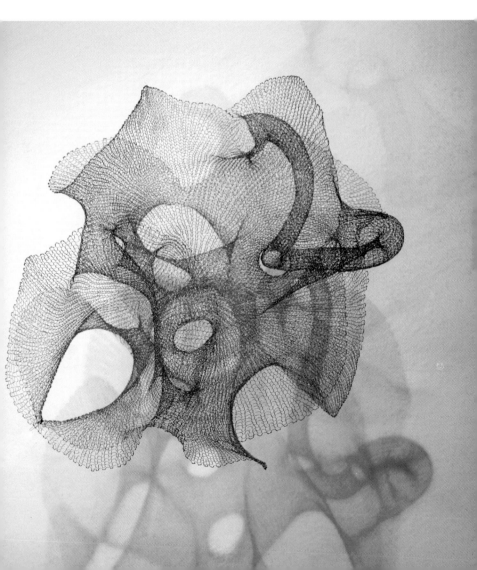

Words

Searching for some words to knit by? Read on! These entries provide plenty of (woolly) inspiration.

81

KNITTED POEM

POETRY SOCIETY

A Poem That's As Big As a House!

In October 2009, to mark the hundredth anniversary of Britain's Poetry Society, a massive and heretofore highly secret project was finally revealed: a "mystery" poem, 43 feet wide and 28 feet long, formed of 12-inch letter squares, knit and crocheted by more than one thousand knitters around the world. And the poem was … (drum roll, please): "In My Craft or Sullen Art" by Dylan Thomas.

"It's a poem about the creative impulse that I thought would resonate equally with knitters, readers, and writers," explains Poetry Society Director Judith Palmer. "I also rather liked that it contained the word *spindrift*, which seemed a good yarn-friendly word. Thomas was a notorious perfectionist, endlessly reworking and unraveling his poems until they gave that impression of effortless simplicity that lies at the core of most great art. He was always photographed wearing rather lovely handknits, and his packing lists for reading tours always listed several scarves, which seemed appropriate. I cleared the idea with Thomas' daughter Aeronwy, and she generously gave us the go-ahead. We'd planned for Aeronwy to unveil the knitted poem, but she died suddenly a few months earlier, which gave the unveiling an extra poignancy."

Thomas' "In My Craft or Sullen Art", bigger than life. © *The Poetry Society 2009*

Profile

THE POETRY SOCIETY

IN THE WORDS OF DIRECTOR JUDITH PALMER

I love poetry. I love knitting. I knew I couldn't be the only person to share that combination of enthusiasms. And I was right! To mark the Poetry Society's centenary, I wanted to think of a fun, grand-scale project that could harness the talents of lots of participants. The idea was to celebrate both components of our name—poetry and society. I'd recently knitted a painting (a joke piece with a picot frame titled *Still Life with Mixed Citrus and Surprised Mule*) so the possibilities of intarsia were definitely mulling around in my head.

I wasn't consciously thinking about it at the time, but I'm pretty sure my subconscious was also being worked on by a fabulous poem by the Welsh poet Gwyneth Lewis called 'How to Knit a Poem.' Like Lewis, I've always been struck by the similarities between knitting and poetry. They share that sense of compression—of intense meaning coiled up tight ready to expand in the mind—of form built up carefully, row by row, line by line—and of course, if you go wrong, you just have to unravel back to the problem and rework it. I also believe that both knitting and poetry capture a meditative capability, opening up an imaginative space in the mind.

The idea for the project, and which poem to knit, arrived at almost the same time. It is by a well-known writer, but isn't stale from overfamiliarity, and crucially it is a poem worthy of being honored by everyone's hard work. It's been a joy getting to know the poem so well while sewing up and arranging those totemic words: moon, nightingales, psalms, lovers, griefs, arms.

We knitted the whole poem—twenty lines plus title, stanza breaks, and author's name. I knitted a pink and green letter U, a number 1, and a coral blank square. Far more people wanted to knit than we had letters to offer, so I limited myself to one character—but then we needed an emergency '1' on the last day, so I literally picked up the only viable scraps of wool to hand, found a really bent old pair of needles, and rustled '1' up in a shadowy corner of my friend's bookshop. The postal workers had been on strike for weeks throughout the project, which meant several 'letters' got held up and gave us a few extra challenges, coordinating a massive international enterprise.

We've all got our favorite squares. There are two crochet squares in the border that I find thrilling. The O in *towering* is a smasher, as is the H in *Dylan Thomas*. The wonderful color combinations that emerge have been a constant surprise. Several contributors were beginner knitters, and we feel as fondly for those tight or gappy squares as we do for the letters that glow with technical brilliance. We asked everyone to think of their favorite poem while they knitted and to write that on a label along with their name—the backs of the squares are often as great as the front, with poems embroidered on the backs—everything from Ginsberg's 'Howl' to Wordsworth's 'Daffodils.'

continued

Members of the Poetry Society knitting team, atop their knitted Dylan Thomas poem. *Photos by Hayley Madden,* © *The Poetry Society 2009*

The templates for our letters were made by Rachael Matthews and Louise Harries of the 'modern haberdashers' Prick Your Finger in London. They mentioned the project on their website, and that must have been how news spread. One of our knitters started a Ravelry group, we set up a Facebook fan page, and they have both been great for bonding all these disparate lone knitters into a warm and wonderful woolen knit-a-poem community. Throughout the summer we posted up a different 'knitting poem of the week' on our website, too, to keep people involved. I think Pablo Neruda's 'Ode to My Socks' might have been the greatest hit.

We unfurled the poem on the piazza of the British Library in London on the morning of October 7, 2009. The weather forecast had been dreadful. Torrential rain was predicted, and everyone told us to postpone. But we kept the faith, and the weather miraculously obliged. On October 8, we then displayed the poem at the Royal Festival Hall. It was too much work to get a whole tour schedule sorted in advance when we were dealing with a handmade object and problem-solving all the way, trying to estimate what the exact dimensions would turn out to be. It toured Swansea in Wales next, then the Victoria Baths in Manchester, then went round ancient churches run by the Churches Conservation Trust. But anyone who has forty feet of space and a love of kniterature should let us know!

In 1976, Circle Press published a print portfolio of Roy Fisher's poem about the knitters of Dent, 'Neighbours we'll not part tonight,' and that had a knitted title page. Roy tells me the same artist knitted a bedspread with a poem on it. Apparently the poet Adrian Henri used to wear a jumper with a poem knitted into the back in the 1970s. But otherwise, ours is a first!"

82
KNITTED POETRY MITTENS

ANONYMOUS

Poems for Your Hands!

In the Textiles collection of the Smithsonian National Museum of American History lie these extraordinary mittens, knitted in the early nineteenth century. *Who* knitted them will perhaps forever remain a mystery. But the *what*, at least, is clearly distinguishable.

Beginning at the bottom of the first mitten, then spiraling to the top, then picking up at the wrist of the second mitten, are the following (rather moralistic) words:

> One thing you must not borrow nor never give away
> For he who borrows trouble will have it every day
> But if you have plenty and more then you can bear
> It will not lighten yours
> if others have a share
> You must learn to be contented then will your trouble cease
> And then you may be certain that you will live in peace
> For a contented mind is a continual feast.

Knitted onto the thumbs is the name William Watson, who is presumably the author of the poem.

The mittens are made of blue and white homespun wool and feature shag at the cuffs, a technique that the museum points out was described as the "new Mode of Knitting" back in 1803. Similar mittens are extant—curiously, some even with the same poem stitched through their fibers. What knitter wouldn't be content to have a pair of his or her own?

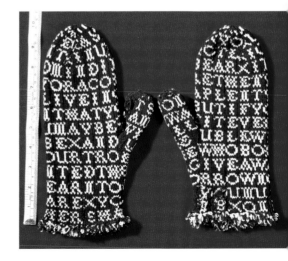

An anonymous knitter's words to live by. *Photo: Smithsonian Institution, National Museum of American History*

83
KNITTING LETTERS: A TO Z— AN ABECEDARIUM

SUSETTE NEWBERRY

Just Like the Real Alphabet!
Only Knitted!

Visitors to Susette Newberry's amazing blog site have been witness to a remarkable project for lo these past several years: the creation of an alphabet in knitting that "celebrates," writes Newberry, each "letter's typographic design and the word that represents it." Thus, in Newberry's fantastic yarn world:

A is an Artichoke design inspired by William Morris motifs.

B is replete with Bohus Stickning patterning.

C is made from Cables.

D is made in the style of Danish Damask.

E is incorporated into what Newberry has dubbed her "Endless Fair Isle Sweater."

F is fashioned from Fair Isle.

G is tucked into the stitches of a Gansey.

H, for History, is a loopy turquoise affair informed by Annemor Sundbo's book *Invisible Threads in Knitting*.

I, for Inspiration, is a long narrow swatch incorporating eyelet columns.

J is two interlocking Js in Centaur font and Italic Swash Caps.

J is for Jacquard. This example features two interlocking Js in Centaur font, and were part of Newberry's experiment to see if she could accomplish the two key elements of jacquard with hand knitting: reversibility and stranding.
Photo © Susette Newberry

K refers to William Morris' Kelmscott Press marks.

L is fuzzy from Lopi.

M is made from the electronic font known as Mantinia.

N, for Nantucket, harkens back to New England Needlework samplers.

O is for the quintessential Fair Isle OXO pattern.

190

P, for Peru, is a set in a striped triangle that looks like the earflap of a *ch'ullu*.

Q is a colorful loop and curl of steely Quatrefoil, the "architectural equivalent to a four-leaf clover."

R is a Red Letter.

S is for Suzani.

T stands for Turkey (the country and its complex knitting tradition, not the holiday bird).

U is for Union Pearl, the seventeenth-century display font that Newberry's blog name riffs on.

V stands for Viking.

W will be colored with Woad;

X is for X-height, which in typography is, technically, the height of the letter x.

Y appears on a sweater Yoke.

Z is for the ornamental penmanship font, Zaner.

And, the pièce de résistance:

& is represented by a black and white repeating-ampersand motif hat.

But remarkable as each of Newberry's knitted letters are in their own right, even more compelling to some of her readers is the extensive history that accompanies each of them—for Suzani, an excursus on the silk road along which the textile originated, the word's etymological origins, and the design motifs that inform it. Did I mention? Newberry's first and foremost occupation is: librarian.

*A version of this entry first appeared in *Twist Collective* Spring 2010.

Q is for Quatrefoil, what Newberry calls the architectural equivalent of the four-leaf clover. A frequent component of gothic church architecture, Newberry's version is an intarsia "stained glass" letter offset by Barbara Walker's quatrefoil cable. *Photo © Susette Newberry*

T is for Turkey—the country, not the holiday bird. From top to bottom, it features horizontal (rather than traditionally vertical) motifs: large and small *boncuk*, or symbols to ward off the evil eye; latticework; hooks; and nightingale's eyes. *Photo © Susette Newberry*

Profile

SUSETTE NEWBERRY

IN HER OWN WORDS

This project actually arose out of two major interests of mine: knitting and the history of the book, especially letterpress printing. Essentially, what I am doing is knitting a book. I'm a librarian, but I also have a Ph.D. in art history, majored in art in college, and own three iron printing presses. When you put all that together, it's not surprising that I'm interested in letterforms and illustration, both of which the abecedarium (or as the British say, abecedary) book genre explores.

I've been interested in abecedaria since I was in college, and have begun collecting examples in recent years. They are generally books for teaching—as in teaching the letters of the alphabet. But

typographers love them for showcasing the design of each letter of the alphabet. Rather than writing and illustrating an abecedarium, I decided to make my own version, bringing in elements of the commonplace book and grounding the project in my combined passions.

For me, the blog and tangible project are inseparable. The blog gives me an opportunity to highlight knitted letters and explore related themes, but more essentially, to bridge virtual and physical fields. I couldn't let my mind wander so freely or go on so many visual adventures without the Internet. And as much as it allows me to roam, it's a way to invite participation from readers who leave comments, are willing to follow links to go on their own virtual journeys, and of course, share tips and resources.

Most of my letters have chosen themselves—except Q, which several readers of my blog suggested. My only guidelines have been that the theme should relate to typography, letterforms, literacy, textiles, or, of course, knitting (cultures of, techniques of, materials of, traditions of). I've always tried to choose a theme that combines as many of the above as possible, and the ideas have generally made obvious choices of themselves (from my perspective, anyway). I haven't tried to make each letter unique, it's just that there's so much to write about that each one seems to be an opportunity to learn more, or explore something new or dear. I haven't devised a pattern for each letter—that's kind of a dream I'd like to be able to do some day; I've really only done three. But I do try to imagine a project for each one.

I research every letter. I'm a librarian! I find research fulfilling; it allows me to discover new images, new books, new ideas, new designs. It's generally the first thing I do, but it continues throughout the design, knitting, and writing phases.

When I began, I generally chose projects I had already made and written about. It wasn't until I was almost halfway through the alphabet that I realized I was actually knitting a book; that I started to look at each new post as a new adventure, rather than an excursion into my past. I'm trying to go back now and reknit some of those early letters into discrete 'pages.' I've already rewritten one letter (B). But I'm hoping to go back after I've completed the alphabet and revisit each letter with an update on the project in question, showing some in their new incarnations.

Each letter has been a completely different time commitment. The first few were pretty easy to write about, didn't involve a lot of research, and, since I wasn't knitting anything new, they took about three or four hours. By the time I got to F and started making videos and knitting enormous swatches (now 'letters') at a tiny gauge, I was devoting more like thirty or forty hours to each one, not getting much sleep, but loving every moment. Since I work full time, I knit at night and on weekends, and until my fingers drop off during holidays.

[Eventually], I'm going to set each letter into a white (knitted) border and make of each a page, then bind them together into a book with a cover, spine, and endpapers. It will be rather thick, of course, but a recognizable codex. Only soft. And woolly.

LACE ALPHABET VEIL

BRIDGET ROREM

A Mother's Love in Every Stitch!

It took knitwear designer Bridget Rorem eleven months to knit the veil for her daughter Ingrid's wedding. If you are thinking, "Eleven months?" Just wait'll you hear the stats.

Constructed of a single, continuous strand of extremely fine Merino on a OOO circular needle, the finished veil was a seamless 76 inches square, composed of 716,582 stitches "give or take a few," as Rorem quipped to *Piecework* magazine; used 3¼ miles of yarn (and yet weighed a mere 8 ounces); and encompassed no fewer than 18 lace patterns, mostly invented by Rorem herself. Perhaps the most impressive feature of all: the messages Rorem knitted to her daughter around the edges of the veil, using an alphabet commonly found in eighteenth-century embroidery samplers: "Ingrid Rorem weds Fulton Gilberth Gale IV," "Fulton Gilberth Gale IV weds Ingrid Rorem," "June twenty-first, nineteen hundred ninety-eight" (the date of the wedding), and the last two lines of "A Drinking Song" by William Butler Yeats. With these facts in hand, one can only wonder why it didn't take Rorem eleven *years* to finish this veil.

Here is a brief tour of the patterns, starting from the center and working outward: a Celtic-style knot; small spruce trees and buttonweeds; orchards of pear trees, with hearts where the branches meet; a diagonally winding creek; ferns, which Rorem designed; pairs of swans, from a Barbara Walker pattern titled "Wings of the Swan"; fields of wildflowers; stepping stones and weeds; baby birds; full-grown spruces; double diamonds; the texts mentioned above; English sunrise motif; branches; rabbits; arches; and finally, a Van Dyke border.

And touching as is all the labor and thought that went into this veil, as well as the physical manifestation that emerged at eleven-months' end, what stands out as the most heartwarming feature is the stories behind the choosing of each and every one of the patterns. They are memories of a mother for the small moments in the girlhood of her beloved daughter, and her fervent wishes for a future of love and happiness.

Tying the Knot

Once upon a time, a girl would knit the contents of her trousseau. These "girls" have knit the whole wedding.

85
WEDDING DRESS

ANGELA YANDEL

Bride Knits Own Gown!

Back in March 2008, Angela Weaser had a dream. The dream was to knit the dress she would wear to marry Dan Yandel a year later. But little did the forty-one-year-old computer programmer know what an odyssey her *intended* project would prove to be.

It started simply enough, with a few skeins of Artyarns variegated silk and a pattern for a ribbed lace corset by Annie Modesitt. But after stitching it up, Weaser experienced that stomach-dropping epiphany familiar to most knitters at one time or another: the top wasn't to her liking—too stripey. She decided to frog it and use the yarn to knit a wrap instead. She found new yarn for the top—Louet Lace Weight Mohair in champagne—and started knitting it all over again. Then, in July, she began work on the biggest chunk of the challenge: the skirt.

"When I first saw the pattern back in March of 2008, and read that the final circumference consisted of 4,800 stitches, I literally thought, 'That's absolutely crazy!' and put the thought out of my mind," she recalls. "But then I saw the Karenknitz wedding dress on Ravelry and began seriously to consider knitting it; she sent me a very enthusiastic reply, plus a bunch of advice that I really appreciated. At this point, the wedding was almost a year away, and I felt like I had all the time in the world."

But by the beginning of May, with 162 rows needed to complete the skirt (also out of laceweight mohair), and a circumference of up to 100 feet, Weaser eventually found herself knitting against the clock—and losing. With ten days to go until the wedding, Weaser had only one choice: to ask for help.

As luck would have it, her favorite Bloomington, Indiana, yarn shop had an optimistic motto: "If you buy your yarn here, we'll help you finish any project." And, true to their word, several women at the shop donated their time to knitting the skirt while Weaser was at work—even picking it up from her office and delivering it back to her at day's end, according to a local newspaper. The skirt was finished the night before the wedding. "My overconfidence came back and bit me when the bind-off"—a make-two picot edge using two strands of mohair—"wound up taking almost forty hours to complete!"

In the end, 314,550 stitches were knitted into the skirt alone, and 4.35 miles of yarn were used to form its gently billowing ruffles. The payoff was a big one. "I absolutely loved wearing my wedding dress," says the now–Mrs. Yandel. "It was more beautiful than I had hoped and felt like the only thing I *could* have worn on this day."

"You may kiss the bride": a big finale for the now–Mrs. Angela Yandel, in her knitted wedding skirt and top. *Photos by Geoff Hughes © 2009 Geoff Hughes Photography, Bloomington, Ill.*

86

KNITTED WEDDING

PUMP HOUSE GALLERY/
CAST-OFF KNITTING CLUB FOR BOYS & GIRLS,
STARRING FREDDIE ROBINS

Even the Vows Were Knitted!

In 2005, artist Freddie Robins (see her *Knitted Homes of Crime*, page 42) co-curated an intriguing exhibition. Titled *Ceremony*, and on view at London's Pump House Gallery, the exhibit merged workshops, projects, and performances all related to the concept of rites of passage. For the pièce de résistance, Robins "married" her already-husband, Ben Coode-Adams—or at least, went through all the motions of the rite. But the real art of the piece was, simply, everything. Because everything was—you guessed it—knitted.

The Cast Off Knitting Club for Boys & Girls provided its members, as well as knitting participants from the general public, patterns for bows, candles, doves, flowers, and

Here comes the bride (artist Freddie Robins). *Photo by Angus Leadley Brown*

sandwiches. But those were only the tip of the proverbial nuptial iceberg. Robin's dress, as well as her bouquet, were knitted. Her train was knitted by a machine-on-wheels as the the ceremony progressed, growing longer and longer as Robins walked down the aisle to say "I do." Even the vows were knitted—says gallery owner Rachael Matthews, "They contained lots of knitting terms and puns and references to knots, and here was a symbolic tying of a knot as part of the ceremony." Coode-Adam's top hat and scarf were, of course, knitted. As were the cameras used by the "paparazzi," the confetti, most of the garments worn by the onlookers, the rings, the champagne, the miniature bride and groom to top the cake, the cake itself and the knife to cut it, the accompanying sweet treats and a salad.

Fortuitously, guests were forewarned to pack their own nonknitted picnic.

The rings. *Photo by Angus Leadley Brown*

A happy bride and groom. *Photo by Angus Leadley Brown*

From top to bottom: Sandwich, anyone? And cake that looks good enough to eat.
Photos by Angus Leadley Brown

87

WEDDING BANQUET

DANIELA EDBURG

Set the Banquet Table with These Knits!

Photographer Daniela Edburg is no slouch when it comes to constructing the sets for her pictures. In the past, she's frosted cakes, sewn dresses, covered foam with *nori* to make monster tentacles, and constructed entrails from Jell-O and velvet. Lately though, "knitting has become the centerpiece of my work."

For *Wedding Banquet*, Edburg knit the flowers and decorations, candlesticks and candles, salt and pepper shakers, ashtrays, forks, spoons, knives, placemats, name cards, and most of the tablecloth. A friend of Edburg's, as well as Edburg's grandmother, crocheted the champagne bottles and cake, wineglasses, plates, napkins, leaves, and vases. Edburg's brother-in-law, a former wedding dress designer, donated a "jinxed" dress of his own devising to the ensemble.

> "The way a single strand of yarn can be shaped into anything with nothing to hold it together but itself, is fascinating."

"The wedding [the dress] was made for was called off twice, and never took place," explains Edburg. "My brother-in-law thought it was amusing that I chose this particular dress, although the story didn't play out in the photo."

The banquet awaits. *Photo by Daniela Edburg, 2009*

"I love looking closely at knitting," says Edburg. "The way a single strand of yarn can be shaped into anything with nothing to hold it together but itself, is fascinating."

Equally fascinating is the scenario that composes the picture. As Edburg sees it, "The banquet is a character in the scene. It has a dialogue with the bride. They have a very strong relationship, which tells a story." However, the knitting itself, considered solo, has a decided power of its own. "You can relate to it firsthand," says Edburg. "Touch it, walk around it, the objects speak to you directly. They are completely open."

And here is the bride at her *Wedding Banquet*, 2009. *Photo by Daniela Edburg, 2009*

88

THE ELIZABETH

JEMMA SYKES FOR BUTCHER COUTURE

Fit for an Actual Queen!

In 2007, British textile designer Jemma Sykes created this astonishing hand-knitted wedding dress for eco-label Butcher Couture. Working with 2.2 pounds (10 kilograms) of organic wool, natural-dyed pink in honor of Breast Cancer Awareness Month, Sykes accomplished what Butcher Couture founder Babou Olengha called "tiers that imitate waves." How did she do it?

"I can tell you that I didn't use a pattern!" exclaims Sykes. "As a textile designer rather than a fashion designer, the fabric and knitted structure dictated the form. So after a period of fabric development exploring stitches, ideas were drawn up, and then the dress was constructed gradually." (Follow the "Making of Elizabeth" at www.butchercouture .com.) Sykes knitted up individual sections of the dress, then later grafted them all together. She explains, "I used an elongated slip stitch to create the laddered effect. Each piece was then manipulated into shape to create the volume required; this technique was then combined with staghorn cables. I like to use traditional, recognizable knitted structures with ones which perhaps aren't so."

Getting married and feeling like you've just gotta have this dress? Never fear! At press time, this dress was still for sale, for a cool £25,000. As a bonus, 30 percent of the sale will be donated to the Breast Cancer Campaign.

The amazing, organic, hand-knit *Elizabeth* dress. *Photo by Butcher Couture*

Bejeweled

Long may these knits sparkle!

89
FABERGÉ EGG

GAYLE ROEHM

Bigger Than Life! You Can Open It!

Gayle Roehm, a former management consultant who now devotes herself to fiber arts, constructed this superlative egg as a contest entry for Meg Swansen's Knitting Camp in 2002. "The theme that year was 'holidays,'" she remembers. "I'm not sure why I tried such an ambitious item, but I decided to make a jewellike egg that opened to reveal a hidden treasure, such as those the Russian tsars' family members had given each other every Easter in the final years of their reign."

Roehm consulted a book called *Fabergé Eggs: Imperial Russian Fantasies*, hoping to find just the right ovum. Says Roehm, "I chose one with details that could (I hoped!) be simplified to show up well in knitted fabric. It's called the 'Spring Flowers Egg,'" which was created sometime before 1899.

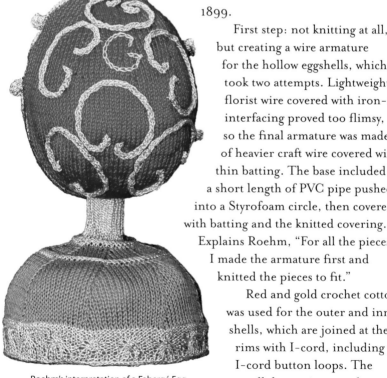

First step: not knitting at all, but creating a wire armature for the hollow eggshells, which took two attempts. Lightweight florist wire covered with iron-on interfacing proved too flimsy, so the final armature was made of heavier craft wire covered with thin batting. The base included a short length of PVC pipe pushed into a Styrofoam circle, then covered with batting and the knitted covering. Explains Roehm, "For all the pieces, I made the armature first and knitted the pieces to fit."

Red and gold crochet cotton was used for the outer and inner shells, which are joined at the rims with I-cord, including I-cord button loops. The scroll decorations on the outer

Roehm's interpretation of a Fabergé Egg, from the outside …

shell are also I-cord. Finally, the flower basket consists of cotton I-cord knitted over floral wire, which allowed Roehm to bend it into shape.

The original egg is described as exhibiting "neorococo gold scrolls and foliage, opening along a vertical diamond-set seam to remove a miniature basket of ... flowers with chalcedony petals and demantoid pistils, the egg fastening at the top by means of a diamond-set clasp." Well, if you can't quite afford the bejeweled original (at least one has sold at auction for upward of $18 million), Roehm's knitted version will certainly do in a pinch!

... and inside, revealing all its intricate charm. *Photos by Miriam Rosenthal, ThirdEyePhotography*

90

JEWELRY

RUTH LEE

Jewelry You Can Knit!

Why should hand-knitters have all the fun? This question must have been on Ruth Lee's mind when she set out to devise a series of neckpiece and bracelet patterns for *Machine Knitting News*. "I wanted to encourage machine knitters to be more adventurous and creative in their approach," recalls Lee. The result was a series of small jewelry pieces that could be made "by the average machine knitter, using readily available materials."

Inspired by her own mandates for other machine knitters, Lee, an associate lecturer at Cumbria Institute of the Arts in Carlisle, UK, went on to make her own jewelry. Using two strands of wire, she knits them at a standard gauge using short rows and other typical shaping techniques. Most of her materials "are not normally associated with knitting," says Lee. The most recent pieces are made of two ends of 0.1mm enameled wire along with one strand of metallic machine embroidery thread.

The result: knitted metal that's actually soft to the touch!

The jewelry of Ruth Lee: a veritable smorgasbord of knitted wiry amorphous forms. *Loop. Photo by Michael Wicks*

From top to bottom: *Ripple,* detail; *Vine*; *Ripple,* unfurled. *Photos by Michael Wicks*

It's Alive!

There's absolutely nothing that knitting (and crochet) can't do. Just ask these animators!

Naturally, you choose natural gas

KNITMATION

MAX ALEXANDER

Knitting That Moves!

London native Max Alexander has been knitting since his twentieth birthday, when "my mum gave me some wool and needles, and I taught myself to knit with a little how-to guide." Only, his goal hasn't been to create static sweaters or sculptures. Alexander's pet fixation is animation. Or, in this case: "knitimation." His website features short videos of knitted critters fighting and dancing and head banging because, "I'd much rather have jokes than seriousness any day!" quips Alexander.

The fun does come with a few technical hurdles, however. The main one is "usually working out how to keep my characters standing upright," says Alexander. "They have simple wire structures inside them which don't always want to behave the way I'd like. It's also quite difficult to reposition the characters without moving their outfits, which usually results in a strange rustling effect." The solution? "I've decided that it's all part of the charm—otherwise I'd go crazy!"

Top: A still from his knitimation video *I Am Ahab*. Bottom: One of Alexander's dastardly knitted creations. *Photos © Max Alexander, maxsworld.co.uk*

WALKIE TALKIE MAN

DIRECTED BY MICHEL GONDRY

Knitted Security Guard Destroys City!

Max Alexander's created a knitted universe all his own. But by far the grandfather of the knitimation genre is a 2004 video directed by Michel Gondry for the New Zealand band, Steriögram. In it, the band is seen recording in a studio while a concert security guard ravages cars and buildings along a city street. Sounds like pretty run-of-the-mill MTV fare. Only, pretty much everything in the video—microphones, reel-to-reel player, movie camera, drums, guitars, buildings, helicopter, and the security guard himself—is knitted. In life size. And sometimes knitted, in triple time, right before your eyes.

Sounds like pretty run-of-the-mill MTV fare. Only, pretty much everything in the video … is knitted. In life size.

All this knitting was led and managed by artist and New York City shop owner Lauri Faggioni, who went on to work on some of Gondry's other projects, including his movie *The Science of Sleep*. You can watch the video on YouTube. Then watch it again. And again.

BRAIN

KATE FENKER

This Is Your Brain on Yarn!

Type "Kate Fenker" into YouTube and what you'll turn up is a 1:50 minute stop-motion movie of a human brain being crocheted into existence. It's weird. It's, well, pretty. And it takes a lot more yarn than you might expect.

In the first year of its airing, *Brain* gained a cult web following—and clamorings for further animated adventures. Which, happily for craft fans, Fenker has big plans to oblige. Flying Brain, anyone?

Fenker's hand-knit *Brain. Photo courtesy of Kate Fenker.*

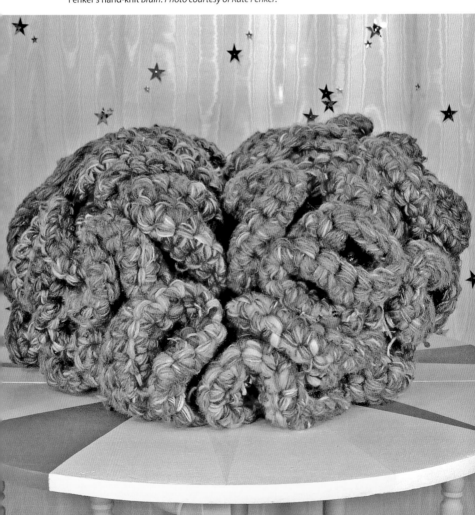

Profile
KATE FENKER
IN HER OWN WORDS

First of all, how did you do it?

KF: It took four weeks to make the brain (it is big—I used twenty pounds of yarn!). But I shot the whole thing in one night, from sundown to sunrise.

I love stop motion, and my first plan was to shoot the frames as I crocheted. I marked the placement of the work, and of the camera, and started out that way. It didn't take long before I realized that it would be way, way better to complete the brain, then shoot frames as I unraveled it, then play it backward. It took 1,351 jpeg images from an ordinary digital camera. To edit, I used iMovie and QuickTime Pro and figured it out as I went along.

What gave you the idea to animate this Brain in the first place? Have you gotten a lot of feedback about it?

KF: You mean like: "Holy Crochet Brains Knitwoman, Fenkerstein's mind has escaped the Metropolis!"—[web designer] Chandler Moss?

Or :

"Parthenogenesis has never looked so good.

the brain is loose!

the aeon of Fenkertech has begun!

i am bewitched and assimilated.

more.

more.

more."—[performance artist] Orji Walflauer

A lot of people have expressed interest in the Brain's further adventures, which I still am cooking up. In one scheme, the Brain flattens into a magic carpet and takes off. In another, it splits into a flock of mini-brains. The Brain really seems to want to get airborne!

To get back to your question, the idea to animate came from scrolling through multiple images of other artwork, and seeing the objects appear to lurch and fidget as the frames went by. I thought,

"Wow, it looks like they are struggling to come to life!" Video also provides a way to make the building process part of the final product. The wildest thing, though, is experiencing the difference between making an object that is seen by very few, and making something that can be experienced directly via popular media. I made *Brain* as a fun, if laborious, experiment—and it ended up getting more attention than I ever imagined.

What were some of the technical challenges in crocheting a brain? Why crochet it rather than, say, knit or sew it?

KF: First, I roughly calculated the progression of numbers of stitches that would result in a solid sphere, then reduced that to a 2/3 sphere, and loosened it up even more to

continued

The progress of a Brain: coming along … all stitched up …

… and going, going, on its way to gone. Photos courtesy of Kate Fenker

allow for the hyperbolic crochet approach (see the entry on Daina Taimina, page 174) at the end, to expand and roll over the outside edges. I also marked a halfway point at both sides, then added extra rows to fill out the back half.

I love knitting, but I chose to crochet the brain for three reasons. One, because one would need a lot of long circular needles to make it around the thousands of fat stitches comprising the convoluted perimeter of the over-30-inch diameter form. Two, crochet lends itself to a stiff chunkiness that was appropriate in this case. Three, you only have one open stitch at a time with crochet, rather than a whole knit row's worth, so it is easy to unravel in a controlled way.

As far as why not sew it (or for that matter, build it out of steel or cookie dough), I wanted to see it grow from the inside out, rather than designing it from the outside in. Also, unlike most building processes including sewing, knitting and crochet are wonderfully reversible—you can totally undo your work back to the yarn you started with. Cool.

Can you please give me a little background about you and how you learned to crochet, when, and why you have applied it to your art?

KF: I learned to knit and crochet in the early 2000s working for Zaldy, the wonderful fashion designer in New York City. At the time, I was reading a lot on biology and evolution and couldn't help making associations between stitches and cells, and applying what I could of organic growth patterns to needlework.

Do you have a particular interest in mathematical formulas and theories?

KF: Yes, math gets to inhabit extra dimensions and has the power to address really weird questions. I envy mathematicians [because] they can work with forms that we can't even conceive of in three dimensions. I dream about that stuff.

94

COMMERCIAL FOR NATURAL GAS BELGIUM

TBWA BRUSSELS, PRODUCED BY LOVO FILMS, DIRECTED BY OLIVIER BABINET

Waking Up to Everything but Knitted Coffee!

This ingenious 37-second spot, which aired on Belgian television, envisions a house waking up in the morning to the warmth of natural gas.

A timer goes off at 7:30 a.m., at which point the boiler kicks in. It begins to spread its heat: across a pipe, up a radiator, over a pair of sneakers, across a tile floor and around a cat basket, up a wall, then a banister, over some

In LOVO's natural gas commercial, the yarny heat creeps up the radiator and over a pair of sneakers ...

... up the walls and banister ...

... all through a child's room ...

Naturally, you choose natural gas

... and ends in the kitchen, with a nice kettle for tea. *Images courtesy of LOVO Films*

striped wallpaper and a painting, over a child's floor-mat city and engulfing some toys and a crib, across a wood-slat floor, out a shower nozzle, and finally, up through a stove burner and tea kettle, to emerge as steam. Playing the role of heat is, you guessed it: knitted and crocheted wool, of course!

The creative team worked for one month to knit all the coverings for these various objects and to set them in place. Large ones, such as the walls and floor, were made by a small knitting manufacturer called Cousy, which specializes in tailor-made knittings, according to LOVO Films. The smaller objects were hand-knitted—and you can catch a glimpse of the craftswomen in the equally riveting spot on the making of the commercial (find both on YouTube). All in all, over 80 kilograms—that's 126 pounds—of yarn was used. Shooting was accomplished in four days, on four cameras. Can you guess how it was done?

Stats

Everyone loves a record-breaker. Here's a round-up of the some the craft world's most impressive.

95

WORLD'S FASTEST KNITTER!

MIRIAM TEGELS

Faster Than a Speeding Bullet (Probably)!

Guinness World Records confirms it: The fastest knitter of all time is Miriam Tegels of the Netherlands, who managed a lightening-swift 118 stitches in one minute flat on August 26, 2006. Using light blue DK weight wool from Lana Grossa, as well as Guinness-mandated 16-inch size 6 (4mm) needles, Tegels stretched out calmly on an orange-striped chaise lounge with her town's mayor and a variety of well-wishers looking on as she shattered the Fastest Knitting record, held for twenty-six years by Brit Gwen Mathewmann, of 111 stitches in a minute.

The forty-five-year-old yoga teacher practiced speed knitting for an hour and a half every day for six weeks, at one point managing an astonishing (and unconfirmed) top speed of 123 stitches in a minute.

How did she do it? The forty-five-year-old yoga teacher practiced speed knitting for an hour and a half every day for six weeks, at one point managing an astonishing (and unconfirmed) top speed of 123 stitches in a minute. At the competition, she reports that she felt a mixture of "excitement, confidence, and anxiety," but that "once all my loved ones got together to cheer me on, my confidence grew."

Confidence-boosting aside, Tegels has five tips for knitting at breakneck speed:

Knit continental.

Keep your shoulders relaxed.

Keep movements small and to a minimum.

Let the yarn drape over your left index finger, and hold it with ring and middle fingers to keep tension.

Practice!

In January 2008, American Lisa Gentry—who holds the Fastest Crocheter in the World title—attempted to break Tegels' record. And she might well have done it; Gentry recorded herself knitting at 119 stitches in a minute. However, due to technical difficulties with her video equipment, she was unable to record the event. And so, as of this writing, Tegels remains the undisputed champion. But for how long? Follow Tegels' tips, and who knows? Perhaps you could become the next Fastest Knitter.

She's a blur: Tegels, the Guinness World Record holder for fastest knitter, knitting fast to break the record. *Photo courtesy of Speedknitter.nl*

96

WORLD'S BIGGEST KNITTING

INGRID WAGNER

Big Enough to Knit You a House!

Have you ever "heard of knitting with pins the size of broom handles?" asks UK knitter Ingrid Wagner. She's more than just curious. As the current world's record holder for big knitting, Wagner (the artist who also spearheaded the *Coat for a Boat* project—see page 115), is a serious proponent of all things knit large. In breaking the Biggest Knitting record in March 2008, she used needles measuring 11½ feet (3.5 meters) made specially for her by a team of designer/ engineers in Newcastle upon Tyne; and her own invention of recycled Big Knit wool yarn (salvaged of newly woven wool fabric that is discarded as waste after being used in industrial weaving) to stitch up a rug. In so doing, she handily beat the previous record, held by Julia Hobson, also of England—who could be seen in publicity photos a year prior to Wagner's attempt wielding needles more than twice her height—stranded loosely together by a swathe of turquoise garter stitch. Wagner herself has since begun knitting with an even huger pair of needles—about 13 feet (4 meters), in length—to raise funds for breast cancer research. "I take the needles to shows and events around the UK where, in return for a £1 contribution to the charity, people can knit a stitch or two," explains Wagner.

"I take the needles to shows and events around the UK where, in return for a £1 contribution to the charity, people can knit a stitch or two."

Knitting this big requires lots of help—lots of *big* help. Wagner, who sat on a stool as she knit the 10 rows of 10 stitches that shattered the Guinness record, was held aloft by the Newcastle Eagles basketball team. She quipped to a local newspaper covering the event: "The only time a woman does need a strong man is when she's handling these giant knitting needles."

Wagner holds aloft her world-record-challenging knitting needles.
Photo © NCJ Media

97

BIGGEST CROCHET HOOK

INGA HAMILTON

Hooking for the Record!

Well, the jury (the *Guinness World Records* jury, that is) had yet to weigh in as of press time. But if all goes according to plan, one day soon Brit Inga Hamilton will be on record as having used the biggest crochet hook of all time.

What's the big holdup? Says Hamilton of her claim with the folks at Guinness: "I'm trying to convince them that setting a world record for the largest usable hook is different from the record they have for the largest crocheted blanket (79 feet by 26 feet or 24 meters by 8 meters). Go figure," she marvels. "It's a bit like comparing the largest pen and the longest letter written."

Hamilton's hopefully winning hook, which measures an impressive 4.8 feet long and weighs in at 24 pounds, was whittled by a man named Jimbo (uh, shouldn't that be *Jumbo*?). It was wielded by Hamilton on Halloween of 2009 in Portland, Oregon, under the auspices of the Crochet Liberation Front. The object of Hamilton's hugely spooky crocheting? A spiderweb, of course.

Hamilton attempts to break the record for using the Largest Crochet Hook. *Photo © rockpool candy/Inga Hamilton*

98
KNITTING WITH THE MOST STRANDS OF YARN

RACHEL JOHN

Strand of Yarn the Size of a Mattress!

And the winner is (or it would be, if she had filed the paperwork): Rachel John, for knitting with one thousand strands of yarn all at once, in October 2006. The British textile artist had a personal mandate, however: Anything she made must have a practical purpose.

So, what can you make with a thousand strands of simultaneously knit yarn? A thick, cushy piece of fabric about the size and weight of a mattress.

John poses with her Extreme Knitting: multiple strands of recycled yarn and needles made from tree trunks.

Honorable 99 Mention
MOST KNITTERS AT ONCE

Much More Than Your Average Knitting Circle!

If the record is accepted by the folks at Guinness, attendees at Sock Summit 2009 in Portland, Oregon, will have shattered the not-so-old record (256, accomplished in July 2009 in Sydney, Australia) by a huge margin: 935 knitters, knitting simultaneously for 15 minutes, each on a Guinness-mandated two needles. Look for it on YouTube.

WORLD'S LONGEST SCARVES

RAY ETTINGER AND SUSIE HEWERR

Long Enough to Keep Ten of You Warm This Winter!

For the longest continuous scarf ever knit by one person, the winner is:

Missourian Ray Ettinger, with his 3,523-foot garment, for which he used a total of 48 skeins of royal blue yarn. And perhaps a bit randomly, Susie Hewerr holds the record for longest scarf knit while running a marathon: nearly 4 feet (1 meter, 20cm).

WORLD'S LONGEST PIECE OF I-CORD

AN UNKNOWN KNITTER

Knitting Nancy Breaks Records!

In 1989, a Kent, England, man took up his Knitting Nancy and started looping. The eventual result: 12.26 miles of knitted cord, more than enough, according to Mary Politkya Bush in a 2007 *Piecework* article, "to stretch up—and back down—Mount Everest." *Guinness World Records* recognized this, er, mountainous feat in 2006.

226

Pattern for a Gingerbread Man

(Makes one front, one back)
Design by Louise Butt, *Simply Knitting*, Future Publishing Ltd., Bath, England

MATERIALS

Patons *Diploma Gold DK* (131 yd/50g DK weight yarn), 1 skein Taupe #06237

Size 6 (4mm) needles or size needed to obtain gauge

Small straight cable needle

Red embroidery thread

Selection of beads/buttons to decorate

INSTRUCTIONS

LEFT LEG

CO 7 sts.
Row 1: Purl.
Row 2: K2tog, k4, kfb.
Rows 3, 5, 7, and 9: Purl.
Rows 4, 6, 8, and 10: K2tog, k4, kfb.
Break yarn, leaving leg on needles.

RIGHT LEG

CO 7 sts.
Row 1: Purl.
Row 2: Kfb, k4, k2tog.
Rows 3, 5, 7, and 9: Purl.
Rows 4, 6, 8, and 10: Kfb, k4, k2tog.
Break yarn.
Slip sts of right leg onto the cable needle, then slip them back on to the needle holding the left leg, so that wrong sides of both legs are on the left needle and facing you.
Rejoin the yarn and purl across both legs.

BODY AND ARMS

Next row: K2tog at both ends of the row.
Next row: Purl.
Starting with a knit row, work 7 rows in St st.
Next row: CO 7 sts, then purl to end.
Next row: CO 7 sts, then knit to end.
Starting with a purl row, work 5 rows in St st.
Next row: BO 7 sts, purl to end.
Next row: BO 7 sts, knit to end.

SHOULDERS AND HEAD

Next row: P2tog at both ends of row.
Next row: K2tog at both ends of row.
Next row: P2tog at both ends of row.
Next row: Kfb at both ends of row.
Next row: Pfb at both ends of row.
Next row: Knit.
Next row: Pfb at both ends of row.
Next row: Knit.
Next row: Purl.
Next row: Knit.
Next row: P2tog at both ends of row.
Next row: K2tog at both ends of row.
Next row: Purl.
Next row: K2tog at both ends of row.
BO purlwise.
Repeat for Back.

continued

TO MAKE UP

Sew on the bead eyes and buttons. Embroider the mouth on the right side, using backstitch and the red embroidery thread.

Sew both pieces of the man together with the right sides facing, leaving an opening on one side so that the man can be turned right side out. Once turned right side out, stuff with polyfill, sew up the opening with mattress stitch.

Add a length of yarn to the back of the man's head so that it can be hung up.

Pattern for a Penguin Jumper

by Marg Healy

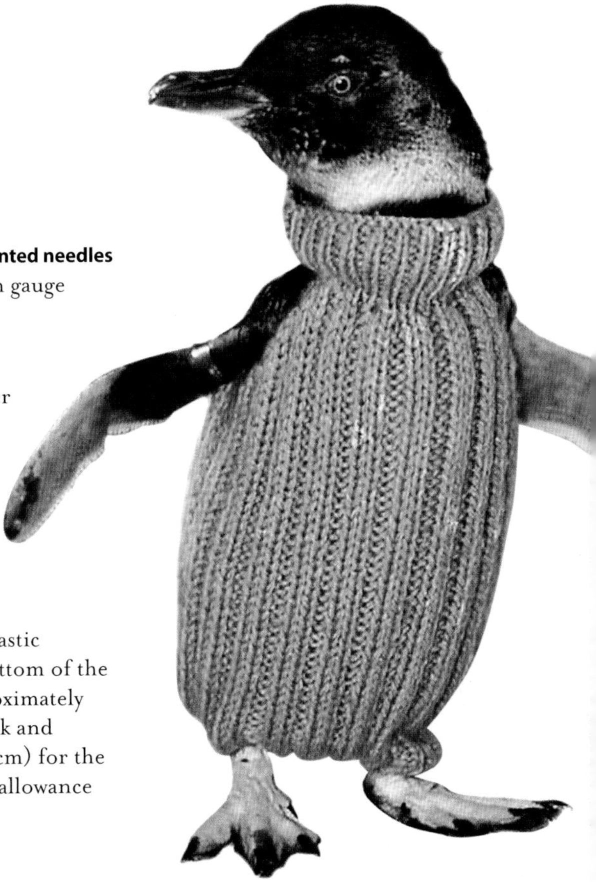

MATERIALS

1 skein DK yarn

Size 9 (5.5mm) needles

Size 11 (8mm) double-pointed needles
or size needed to obtain gauge

PATTERN NOTES

If you are a loose knitter, use smaller needles. The sweater must be firmly knit to keep the penguins from taking them off.

Penguins are experts at removing unwanted covering; therefore, thread hat elastic through the top and bottom of the finished sweater—approximately 6.7" (17cm) for the neck and approximately 7.5" (19cm) for the bottom. We have made allowance for a small knot.

INSTRUCTIONS

CO 36 sts.
Work k1, p1 ribbing to end of row.
Rep for 7 more rows.
Change to k2, p2 ribbing and inc 1 st at end of this and the next 4 rows—44 sts.
Cont until work measures approx 6" (15cm).
Dec 1 st end of each row until 28 sts rem.
Dec 1 st in middle of next row—27 sts.
Leave sts on the needle.
Make 2nd side same as first.
With double-pointed needles, knit 18 sts onto 3 needles.
Work k1, p1 ribbing for 16 rows.
BO.
Stitch up sides to beg of dec to 27 sts (opening for each flipper).

Pattern for a Helmet Liner

by Cat Mazza

MATERIALS

260 yd DK weight 100% wool yarn in black, brown, or gray

Size 6 (4mm) 16" circular needle

Size 6 (4mm) double-pointed needles (set of 4)

Stitch marker

INSTRUCTIONS

NECK

Using double-pointed needles, CO 84 sts. Use a stitch marker to mark the beg of the rnd.

Rnd 1: K2, p2 to end of rnd.

Rep Rnd 1 until piece measures 6".

EYE ACCESS

Next rnd: From marker, continue k2, p2 rib for 26 sts, then BO 32 sts, cont in k2, p2 rib for rem 26 sts.

FOREHEAD

Next rnd: From marker, continue in k2, p2 rib for 26 sts, CO 32 sts, then continue in k2, p2 rib to end of rnd.

Next rnd: K2, p2 to end of rnd. Rep this rnd for 1".

Next rnd: Knit. Rep this rnd for 3".

CROWN SHAPING

Switch to 4 double-pointed needles

Rnd 1: K8, k2tog.

Rnd 2: Knit.

Rnd 3: K7, k2tog, rep to end of rnd.

Rnd 4: Knit.

Rnd 5: K6, k2tog, rep to end of rnd.

Rnd 6: Knit.

Rnd 7: K5, k2tog, rep to end of rnd.

Rnd 8: Knit.

Rnd 9: K4, k2tog, rep to end of rnd.

Next rnd: Cont dec 6 or so sts

Cont. in pattern, K3, K2tog; K2, K2tog; K1, K2tog, K2tog until there only 6 sts remaining.

FINISHING

Pull yarn through loops, use crochet hook or thick needle to tighten from inside, and weave in all ends.

Knit a Crane for Peace

by Seann McKeel

MATERIALS

US 10½ straight needles

Light worsted-weight wool that will felt easily (use up scrap!); Lamb's Pride works great and makes about eight cranes per skein

Darning needle and a bit of contrasting yarn or row marker

Approximate Measurements: Before felting, 12"; after felting 9"

NOTES ON THIS PATTERN

To knit your cranes, begin at the head, then make the neck, then the body/wings, and end with the tail. Finished, each crane is a single piece of fabric that is then felted by hand or in the washing machine. Once felted, the crane is punctured with a darning needle and sewn with leftover yarn to yield its "folded" shape—creating the likeness of an origami crane. This is the unadorned, very basic crane pattern. Cranes can be embellished with different colored yarns or embroidered to look as interesting and beautiful as Japanese origami paper!

WORK HEAD FIRST

TRIANGLE SHAPE

R1: tie slip knot, *co1 = 2 st
R2: k2, co1
R3: p3, co1
R4: k4, co1
R5: p5, co1
R6: p
*cast-on method is yarn over thumb

WORK NECK

RECTANGLE SHAPE

*R7: p2, k2, p2
R8: k2, p2, k2
(continue from *R7 and R8 for 16 rows until there are 24 rows from cast-on edge

WORK BODY/WINGS

R25: co5, mark end of row with scrap yarn
R26: p1, k10, co5, mark end of row with scrap yarn
R27: k1, p14, k1

INCREASE ROWS TO SHAPE SLOPING "TRIANGLE" OF THE WINGS

R28: co2, k2, p1, k14, p1
R29: co2, p2, k1, p14, k1, p2
R30: co2, k4, p1, k14, p1, k2
R31: co2, p4, k1, p14, k1, p4
R32: co2, k6, p1, k14, p1, k4
R33: co2, p6, k1, p14, k1, p6
R34: co2, k8, p1, k14, p1, k6
R35: co2, p8, k1, p14, k1, p8

DECREASE ROWS TO SHAPE "TRIANGLE" OF THE WINGS

R36: bo2, k5, p1, k14, p1, k8
R37: bo2, p5, k1, p14 k1, p6
R38: bo2, k3, p1, k14, p1, k6
R39: bo2, p3, k1, p14, k1, p4
R40: bo2, k1, p1, k14, p1, k4
R41: bo2, p1, k1, p14, k1, p2
R42: bo7, k9, p1, k2
R43: bo7, p5

continued

WORK TAIL

*R44: k2, p2, k2
R45: p2, k2, p2
(continue from *R44 and R45 for 8 more rows)

TRIANGLE SHAPE OF TAIL

R54: bo1, p2, k2
R55: bo1, k2, p1
R56: bo1, p2
R57: bo1, k1
R58: k2tog, bo last st

FELTING

Remove st markers and place crane in a lingerie bag; set washing machine on hot/cold, low water level, and maximum agitation. Add a small amount of laundry detergent and a pair of jeans. Run the crane through a couple of cycles until felted nicely, or felt by hand running alternate hot/cold water on the crane with a little detergent and agitating the fabric. (It works great!)

SHAPING AND "FOLDING"

After you felt the crane, shape it by creasing the neck, head, tail, and wings. Once in this folded fashion, using a darning needle and scrap yarn, sew the neck and tail to the wings. Then tack down the head in a similar manner. You may have to fuss and pull the fabric to get it into shape, but the beauty of felting is that you can manipulate it in this way.

ABBREVIATIONS USED IN THIS PATTERN

R = row	**st** = stitch	**co** = cast on
k = knit	**p** = purl	**bo** = bind off

co stitch is yarn over thumb method

k2tog = knit 2 stitches together

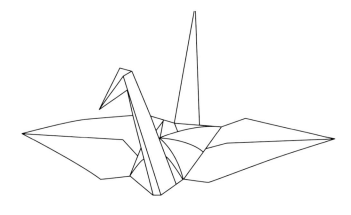

Pattern for Swine Flu (Influenza A Subtype H1N1)

by Clare Dyer-Smith

Here's a pattern for the timeliest microbe of the era. The swine flu virus is round, with two different proteins (HA, haemagglutin, which binds the virus to the cells, and NA, neuaminidase, which helps the virus to multiply) covering the surface. HA and NA are represented in this pattern by beads.

SPECIAL TECHNIQUE

Place Bead: Bring yarn to front and slip the next st as if to purl. Slip a bead close to the right needle, then cont knitting the next st.

MATERIALS

1 skein DK or Aran weight yarn, in color of your choosing

4 double-pointed needles in a size suitable for the yarn weight you are using. I recommend using needles a size or two smaller than the yarn calls for, to produce a firm fabric.

Toy stuffing, such as polyfill

Yarn needle

60 beads in two different colors or shapes—for greater accuracy you will need 3 to 4 times as much of one bead (HA) as of the other (NA)

PATTERN NOTE

Make sure that the holes in the beads you choose are large enough to accommodate the yarn.

INSTRUCTIONS

Thread the 60 beads onto the yarn, in any order you like, using the yarn needle.

CO 6 sts using your preferred method. Distribute sts over 3 double-pointed needles and join to work in the round, being careful not to twist sts. Knit 1 rnd.

INCREASE RNDS

Rnd 1: Kfb 6 times—12 sts.
Rnd 2: (K1, place bead, K2) 3 times.
Rnd 3: (K1f&b, k1) 6 times—18 sts.
Rnd 4: Knit.

Rnd 5: (K1f&b, k2) 6 times—24 sts.
Rnd 6: (K1, place bead, k2) 6 times.
Rnd 7: (K1f&b, k3) 6 times—30 sts.
Rnd 8: Knit.
Rnd 9: (K1f&b, k4) 6 times—36 sts.
Rnd 10: (K1, place bead, K2) 9 times.
Rnd 11: (K1f&b, k5) 6 times—42 sts.
Rnd 12: Knit.
Rnd 13: (K1f&b, k6) 6 times—48 sts.
Rnd 14: (K1, place bead, k2) 12 times.

continued

Rnds 15–17: Knit.
Rnd 18: (K1, place bead, k2) 12 times.
Add stuffing up to just below the level of needles.
Work dec rnds, adding stuffing as you go.

DEC RNDS

Rnd 19: (K2tog, k6) 6 times— 42 sts.
Rnd 20: Knit.
Rnd 21: (K2tog, k5) 6 times— 36 sts.

Rnd 22: (K1, place bead, k2) 9 times.
Rnd 23: (K2tog, k4) 6 times— 30 sts.
Rnd 24: Knit.
Rnd 25: (K2tog, k3) 6 times— 24 sts.
Rnd 26: (K1, place bead, k2) 6 times.
Rnd 27: (K2tog, k2) 6 times— 18 sts.
Rnd 28: Knit.
Rnd 29: (K2tog, k1) 6 times— 12 sts.
Rnd 30: (K1, place bead, k2) 3 times.
Rnd 31: K2tog 6 times—6 sts.

FINISHING

Cut yarn and thread through 6 rem sts (add more stuffing if required). Weave in ends.

Copyright © 2009 Clare Dyer-Smith. You may make copies of this pattern and knit it up for personal use, as gifts, or for charity. You may not sell microbes knitted from this pattern for profit. Contact knittedmicrobes@googlemail.com for more information, for pattern support, or if you spot any mistakes! Enjoy, and remember to always wash your hands!

Abbreviations

beg	begin, beginning, begins		**RH**	right-hand
BO	bind off		**rib**	ribbing
CC	contrast color		**rnd(s)**	round(s)
ch	chain		**RS**	right side (of work)
cm	centimeter(s)		**rev**	sc reverse single crochet
CO	cast on			(crab st)
cont	continue, continuing		**sc**	single crochet
dc	double crochet		**sl**	slip, slipped, slipping

dec(s) decrease, decreasing, decreases

dpn double-pointed needle(s)

est establish, established

inc(s) increase(s), increasing

k knit

k1f&b knit into front then back of same st (increase)

k1-tbl knit 1 st through back loop

k2tog knit 2 sts together (decrease)

kwise knitwise (as if to knit)

LH left-hand

m(s) marker(s)

MC main color

mm millimeter(s)

M1 make 1 (increase)

M1k make 1 knitwise.

M1p make 1 purlwise

pat(s) pattern(s)

p purl

p1f&b purl into front then back of same st (increase)

p1-tbl purl 1 st through back loop

p2tog purl 2 sts together (decrease)

pm(s) place marker(s)

psso pass slip st(s) over

pwise purlwise (as if to purl)

rem remain(s), remaining

rep(s) repeat(s), repeated, repeating

ssk [slip 1 st knitwise] twice from left needle to right needle, insert left needle tip into fronts of both slipped sts, knit both sts together from this position (left-leaning decrease)

ssp [slip 1 st knitwise] twice from left needle to right needle, return both sts to left needle and purl both together through back loops (left-leaning decrease)

st(s) stitch(es)

St st stockinette stitch

tbl through back loop

tog together

w&t wrap next stitch then turn work (often used in short rows)

WS wrong side (of work)

wyib with yarn in back

wyif with yarn in front

yb yarn back

yf yarn forward

yo yarn over

* repeat instructions from *

( ) alternate measurements and/or instructions

[ ] instructions to be worked as a group a specified number of times

Where to Find the Contributors

Max Alexander and his knitimation maxsworld.co.uk

Pat Ashforth, Steve Plummer, and their Woolly Thoughts
woollythoughts.com

M'Lou Baber *Double Knitting: Reversible Two-Color Designs*,
Schoolhouse Press, 2008

Isabel Berglund isabelberglund.dk

Patricia Bown patricia-bown.com

Dave Cole www.theknittingmachine.com

Althea Crome www.bugknits.com

Désirée de Baar desireedebaar.nl

Annelies de Kort anneliesdekort.nl

Andy Diaz Hope andydiazhope.com

Daniela Edburg www.danielaedburg.net

Iris Eichenberg iriseichenberg.nl

Kate Fenker www.katefenker.com

gelitin and their *Hase* gelitin.net

Inga Hamilton www.rockpoolcandy.typepad.com

Jimini Hignett howtogoon.com

Andy Holden www.andyholdenartist.com

Theresa Honeywell theresahoneywell.com

Anna Hrachovec mochimochiland.com

I Knit iknit.org.uk/knitariver.html

JafaBrit (*Knit Knot Tree*) jafabrit.blogspot.com

Marianne Jorgensen marianneart.dk

KnitMinder quilt2go.com/content/knitminder

Bauke Knottnerus and his Phat Knits baukeknottnerus.nl

Lendorff.Keywa and Office Lendorff
www.officelendorff.com

Ruth Lee *Contemporary Knitting for Textile Artists*, Batsford, 2008

Robyn Love robynlove.com

Ode Marie odemarie.blogspot.com

Cat Mazza and Stitch for Senate www.stitchforsenate.us

Debbie New *Unexpected Knitting*, Schoolhouse Press, 2003

Susette Newberry unionpurl.blogspot.com

Mark Newport www.marknewportartist.com

Kate Pokorny and her crocheted yurt yurtalert.com

Maria Porges mariaporges.com

Lauren Porter and her knit Ferrari
www.lauren-porter.co.uk

Alasdair Post-Quinn and FallingBlox www.fallingblox.com

Pump House Gallery pumphousegallery.org.uk

Helen Pynor helenpynor.com

Joanna Ratcliffe and *Bigsock* big-sock.blogspot.com

Freddie Robins www.freddierobins.com

Laurel Roth loloro.com

Magda Sayeg and KnittaPlease magdasayeg.com

Sailors' Society www.sailors-society.org

Emily Stoneking www.emilystoneking.com

Annette Streyl streyl.net

Leslie Sudock and her knitted Seder
tikkunknits.wordpress.com

Daina Taimina *Crocheting Adventures with Hyperbolic Planes*,
AKPeters, 2009; www.math.cornell.edu/dtaimina

Miriam Tegels speedknitter.nl

Jan ter Heide, Evelein Verkerk, and The Knitted Landscape
knittedlandscape.com

Ingrid Wagner www.ingridwagner.com

Patricia Waller www.patriciawaller.com

Tatyana Yanishevsky and *The Knit Garden* knitplants.com

Index

About the Author

Lela Nargi is the author of numerous books, some of them about knitting. The first of these, *Knitting Lessons: Tales from the Knitting Path*, documented her adventures in learning to knit and featured interviews with knitters around the country. Since then, she's published *Knitting Through It: Inspiring Tales for Times of Trouble*, *Knitting Memories*, as well as a slew of essays and articles for magazines and other people's books. She's currently writing a knitting history for Voyageur Press. Lela lives and knits in Brooklyn, NY, with her daughter, her husband, and her dog. Visit her at www.lelanargi.com.